Kinky Christian Sex:

Theology, Ethics and Practical
Advice for Erotic Spanking

Vivian MacKenzie

Kinky Christian Sex: Theology, Ethics and Practical Advice for Erotic Spanking
Copyright © 2020 Vivian MacKenzie

Published by **Comyn Publishing**
Seattle, WA

Some names and identifying details have been changed to protect the privacy of individuals.

ISBN: 978-1-7342301-8-5

Dedicated to my wonderful husband, with immense gratitude for the safety and love he's always shown me around my most tender issues. And to everyone out there that has travelled this road – this crazy, difficult and bewildering road.

Table of Contents

Introduction

1. Spanking as an Orientation
    a. Self-Acceptance
    b. Core Question: Why?
    c. We Are Jesus to Each Other
    d. Myths About Kink Written by Christians
    e. What You do with It
    f. Common Behaviors of Young

2. A Theology of Sin and Sex
    a. Truths About Sex
    b. Truths About Sin
    c. Is Kink a Sin?

3. Kink and Psychology
    a. Kink as a Paraphilia
    b. Kink in the Therapy Office

4. What About Feminism?
    a. BDSM as Ritualized Violence
    b. Feminism and the Sex-Positive Movement
    c. Feminism and Ethical Expression

5. Why Are You Kinky?
    a. Sigmund Freud and the Childhood Spanking
    b. It Must Be Trauma
    c. Because Science
    d. Guilt
    e. Mental Illness

      f.   Kink as an Orientation
6. Making Friends with Your Kink
      a.   The Genie in the Bottle
7. Pop Culture Myths
      a.   Consent Is Merely a Yes
      b.   Kink Always Comes from Trauma
      c.   Kink Can Be "Cured"
      d.   Kink Always Involves Sex
      e.   BDSM Is the Same as Sexual Sadism
      f.   All Kinks Are Pretty Similar
      g.   You Can Tell Who's into Kink
8. Unhealthy Kink
      a.   Questions for Healthy Kink
      b.   Righteous Expression
      c.   Children
9. Christian Domestic Discipline
10. Spanking While Being Single
      a.   Denial and Suppression
      b.   A Rich Fantasy Life
      c.   Self-Spanking
      d.   Finding Someone to Spank You
11. Coming Out
      a.   Your Intimate Partner
      b.   Telling Others
      c.   Writing Fanfiction
12. Sexual Response
      a.   The Link of Kink and Sex
      b.   Types of Orgasms
      c.   BDSM as a Non-Sexual Practice
      d.   Anal Sex
      e.   Oral Sex
      f.   Toys
13. Nuts and Bolts of a Spanking

     a.   Safety

     b.   Spanking Positions

     c.   Spanking Target

     d.   Typical Spanking Protocol and Sexual Response

     e.   Spanking Implements

     f.   Ambiance

     g.   Noise Issues

14. Glossary

15. Bibliography

Intro

This is the hardest thing I've ever written in my life, but I'm going to claim the promise that the truth sets you free. So, I'm going to endeavor to tell the truth to the best of my knowledge, as well as I can. There is freedom in the pen, both for me, the writer, and you the reader, as we can take this journey together. Fear and shame need isolation to fester; connection breaks that isolation. I spent the first part of my life seeking that isolation because I thought of myself as a freak - and I thought that fear and shame were what I deserved. I didn't know that there could be something different until I began to really believe in love, trust, and connection - but in a whole different way than I thought it would look like. If I had found the proverbial genie in the bottle for any part of my first forty years of life, one of my three wishes would have been to take my desire to be spanked out of my head in its entirety. I didn't want it, I didn't need it, and I lived in constant fear of its discovery.

I have, at different times of my life, been a scientist, a pastor, a mother, a wife, and I am now a psychotherapist. I am completely in love with Jesus and teach the children in my Sunday School class that He likes nothing better than forgiving them and changing their lives. I am older than Beyoncé and younger than Oprah, with more children than is strictly respectable, and have been happily married since my late twenties. I am white, cis-gendered, straight, and I come from a rural background but now live in a mid-sized, liberal US city. If you passed me in the grocery store or on the bike path, you wouldn't look twice at me, assuming my plump middle-aged self lived a boring life. But what you don't know about me is that I have a rich fantasy life, so rich in fact that I can't remember the last time I was bored. I don't get bored; I always have a running story going in my head that I'm working on refining. And what those fantasies involve would shock most people. Although if you're reading this book, maybe it wouldn't shock you as much as it would the person reaching for broccoli beside me in the grocery store.

This book is going to be about erotic spanking and what this particular sexual kink has to do with people who are practicing Christians. I'm going to try and write the book I wish I had the opportunity of reading at the beginning of my journey, in the hope of giving encouragement and freedom to my sisters and brothers who are in the same boat as I am. Because there is freedom, there is the truth, and there is a loving God who didn't make a mistake when He created you.

There is a danger when you talk about one particular kink that this could be generalized to other kinks, but I am specifically going to stay away from this sort of generalization. There are sexual deviancies to which there are no acceptable expressions in this world, and for people who have those deviancies, I pray that they find peace. However, I feel like it would be the height of arrogance to discuss a fetish or sexual orientation that is not my own. So, I am not going to talk about any sexualities that are not my own, ones that nearly everyone agrees are harmful such as pedophilia, nor ones that are relatively common and relatively accepted in our society such as homosexuality. I am also not going to address the spanking of children, which is a completely different issue and not at all the issue covered by this book. This book will talk about spanking fantasies and spanking realities between consenting adults.

Chapter 1:
Spanking as an Orientation

"And he whipped Laura with the strap." Those words were emblazoned on my brain when I was a six-year-old in first grade, my earliest memory of reading a book in which there was a spanking. It was from the book *The Little House in the Big Woods* by Laura Ingalls Wilder,[1] and I couldn't explain how or why my body responded to reading that part of the story. My little six-year-old self read that line in the story, and I discovered that my pulse sped up, my breath shortened, and my stomach felt as if it were full of butterflies. I didn't know why that particular scenario did that to me, but I quickly realized that I was the only one around me that had that reaction. The loneliness of the moment when I realized that I was different closed in - I didn't yet have language for the shame and the isolation that I would encounter as I grew up. I didn't want to actually be spanked - I had only been spanked by my parents a few times in my childhood and studiously avoided it at all costs - but there was something incredibly attractive about the fantasy of it. The few stories I read and a few scenes from television soon became the bulk of my fantasy life, and as I began to be able to write, I started writing stories to reflect my fantasy life.

Spanking for me started as an intense interest when I was very young, but it didn't occur to me that it might be sexual for many years. Thinking about it and reading about it caused an intense reaction in my body, but it felt like something intense and pleasant in my stomach and a tingling in my hands and feet, which felt very different than when I thought about sex. Starting in adolescence, I had sexual fantasies as well, and sometimes those fantasies crossed over, but that crossover was rare and had to do with the subject that was being spanked. If I pictured myself as a child being spanked, there wasn't a sexual component at all, but if I pictured myself as a grown woman being spanked, then sometimes there was a sexual component, but usually not. The stories I wrote were chaste; the spankers were always parents or teachers, and the spankees were always children. It wasn't until I was in my forties that I even realized there could be an actual sexual side to my attraction to spanking.

Attraction to spanking or other forms of bondage, discipline, sadism, and masochism (usually shortened to BDSM) for some people, can be a sexy fun thing to do to spice up their sex life. For other people, like me, it is something that has felt like a part of their identity since their earliest memories. Scientists have thought over the years that BDSM was everything from just a sexy activity, or mental illness, or criminal behavior. But more recently, scientists are finding that practitioners of BDSM have more in common with a diverse sexual orientation - including having this interest from an early age, psychological consequences in trying to suppress it, and a pervasive and lifelong pattern. More and more researchers are starting to think of BDSM as an orientation rather than a hobby or an activity.[2]

I first came across this idea when reading a book called *Sex With Shakespeare*, and as I read the author's words, it seemed like they were from my own head and heart. She looked up "spank" in the dictionary when she was a child just like I had done, she knew she was different from an early age, and she had fantasized about it for her whole childhood. But, when she said that her need to read spanking stories drove her to read fanfiction that could be classified as illegal in a cyber cafe when she was in a dangerous area in Afghanistan where she was working as a foreign correspondent,[3] I felt like I had found a kindred spirit. My desire and need to read these types of stories would have done the same thing to me.

This book is going to be about people like me - people who have felt this pull of an off-center kink since early childhood. There are so many terms that have been used derogatorily about people like us for so many years, making people with harmless proclivities sound like scary psychopaths. But the words have a history of hurt - sexual deviancy, fetish, abusive, dark, twisted, sick. A word like "sexual deviancy" should be a neutral word - it should be a word that can be used like math, with some people's point of experience a certain measure of deviant (or spaced from) the norm, or most common.

But after a lifetime of hearing the word "deviant" as meaning sick, twisted and wrong, it is not a word I can use in this book. I likewise dislike the term "fetish" because it brings up the Freudian psychotherapists who coined it and thought they could "cure" it. Some people in this community use the word "spanko," but this has never resonated with me, perhaps because it sounds a little bit like something you might order at a Mexican restaurant or a supportive undergarment. The word I like and use is "kinky," or "spicy," because both of those words imply that people with this particular proclivity are normal people that just have something added extra - added spice to a normal psyche.

What if we could view people who liked kink with as little judgment as we view people who put hot sauce on their burrito? The most surprising things that modern research has found about people who are into kinky things is that it is the psychological equivalent of hot sauce - they have found no link between people who practice BDSM and any psychological problems, and researchers were surprised to find out just how well-adjusted and psychologically healthy they are.[4]

Self-Acceptance

My self-acceptance has been hard-fought, and even then, the people that I have shared this part of myself with can be counted on one hand. It reminds me of how many women struggle with self-acceptance of their hair. Straight, wavy, curly, kinky - whatever hair texture chances are, there was a time in your life that you fought against it with perms, a flat iron, a blow dryer, etc. Peace comes for women when they accept the hair that they have and work within the hairstyles that work for that hair. If a woman has a really curly hair, she can waste hundreds of dollars and hours of her time trying to make her hair look straight - or she can accept that she has curly hair and then decide how she operates from there. She can shave her head, wear braids, learn good products for curly hair, or find a fun short style that shows her curls to their best advantage.

Just as this is true of a woman and her hair, this is true of our basic identities. I fought against this being my core identity for most of my life, wishing and praying for this to not be who I was. If I had found a genie in a bottle, one of my three wishes would have been to take this desire from me. Though I grew up in a small town in a fairly sheltered environment, I knew that this deep part of me wasn't acceptable.

I was walking into my eighth grade English class, and kids were goofing around and, because the teacher was a little late to class, talking about what comes naturally to curious eighth-graders - sex.

"Did you see that movie?" one kid asked. "You know, with the wax museum? Do you think that some people really do like getting beaten during sex?"

"It seems so silly!" A girl from my church laughed. "Like, beat me, beat me? Oh, it's so sexy?"

My heart turned to ash. I knew they were talking about me. I had seen the movie too, and I had felt a strange kinship with the girl in the movie that had been enthralled with the Marquis de Sade - and had become aroused with being beaten. And I knew that if the other people in my class could read my mind, I would be a hated outcast. But it was also hard for me because I didn't necessarily understand my interest in spanking as a sexual thing either - for me, it felt intense but not necessarily sexual. I had a desire for sex as well, but spanking seemed like a separate thing. And I didn't identify with what looked like sadomasochism in the popular culture - leather and whips and chains looked off-putting and scary for me.

And so I grew up, swearing that I would never tell another person of my secret, writing my secret stories and wishing, hoping that something would change. Maybe I would grow out of it? Maybe when I got married and had kids? Surely, nobody that had kids would still write stories with spanking in them.

Core Question: Why?

One core question that all kinky people have at some point is why they are like they are. When I went to college and first had access to scientific periodicals, this was the first question I researched, even though my major in human biology made researching this a bit of a stretch. I spent many wintery Saturdays in the stacks of the University's books and periodicals and found myself no closer to any answers. No scientist has found a link to an interest in BDSM with abuse, trauma, or anything else in childhood. Some kinksters were spanked as children, and some weren't. Some had trauma, but at about the same percentage as the rest of the population. Given that most of the time, people realize this about themselves when they are so young, it seems almost like something that is either present in a child's brain at birth or happens in the first few years.

For ten years after college, I worked as a pastor, hoping for a spiritual victory over my "problem." I confessed, prayed, fasted, read scripture, and hoped for transformation. I burned my stories and forced myself to stop writing new ones, though I couldn't stop the fantasies in my head, and not writing them down made them far more unmanageable. In fits of weakness, I would write stories on my laptop just to get them out of my head, and then erase them. I identified with Paul having a "thorn" in his side, and thanking God for having a secret shame that kept me humble. But no victory came, even with my marriage to my loving husband. And my husband and I took sin very seriously in our walk with God.

Though we had both dated before we met each other, both of us entered marriage as virgins. We even saved our first kiss until our engagement and regularly talked about how to honor God with our choices, with our lives, and with our bodies. We wanted our marriage, and our sex life together, to not have any of the complications that can come from guilt and shame that comes from past sexual baggage. But even though I looked like the perfect blushing bride from the outside, I entered marriage with a secret I intended never to tell. Even though he was an equal partner, and I loved and trusted him, I could not tell him my secret. Part of it was that I hoped my secret would go away, and part of it was that I was so fearful of rejection. The love pats he gave me on the bottom on occasion were so wonderful, what if he realized how much I craved them? Would he agree that I was as dark and twisted as I thought that I was?

We Are Jesus to Each Other

I once went to a wedding where the pastor told the couple that a marriage of faith meant that you got to be Jesus to each other; that in many ways, your spouse is a deep incarnation of Jesus to you. The bible says that all believers can be incarnational representatives of Christ to each other; in a very real way, what we do unto the least of others we do unto Jesus. I believe that the Catholic tradition of confession grew out of our complete inability as humans to wrap our brains around the fact that God loves to forgive us, and it is reassuring to have another human being to stand in His place and assure us that yes, He forgives us. The call on our lives as Christians is to be God's hands and feet in the world, doing His work, and showing His love to people. And, I believe that this is even more so with our spouses. So what I'd had trouble believing the bible about myself - how much God loved me for me, for instance, not for what I produced - I began to believe of my husband, which made it easier to believe of God. A good marriage can be very healing.

So was my new fantasy of having my husband spank me, was this hot and allowable? Or sacrilege, like picturing Jesus spanking me? And that's one of the funny things about transformation - it often doesn't look like what you think it's going to look like. I wonder if the caterpillar knows what the butterfly is going to look like. I assumed that the transformation of me becoming a better Christian would look like me becoming "normal," me becoming the normal suburban housewife whose "spiciness" in her sex life would be trying a different position or using whipped cream. But I was to find out that in God's creation, transformation always has what it is to become within the original. The caterpillar becomes a butterfly, and the butterfly has parts of the caterpillar still in it. Transformation doesn't mean becoming something I'm not; it means redeeming something that I already am. The work God had to do on my heart was not making me into something I wasn't; it was making me into a redeemed version of something I already was. And for me, that transformation looked like a combination of my husband and Harry Potter fanfiction.

But before we go there, I want to talk about the arguments that people use against kink as an orientation and identity. If you Google "BDSM and Christianity," you will get a slew of answers from a range of people. There are a few people that say God made sex to be fun, and what happens between consenting adults is up to them, but those voices are few and give fairly shallow, one- or two-sentence answers. The bulk of the answers, given by experts with psychological and theological degrees alike, condemn the practice. With much self-care and prayer, I have sorted through their arguments and would like to present them here not as arguments against practicing BDSM, but as an underlying misunderstanding of kinky as an orientation that is largely unchangeable.

Myths About Kink Written by Christians:

Kink is abuse because if you did these acts without consent, this would be abuse. Yes, this is true, but so are a lot of other things. The act of going into my friend's house would be breaking and entering without consent, and the beautiful act of marital sex would be rape without consent. Consent tends to change a lot of things.

Women are coerced into this lifestyle, no woman would want to participate if she weren't feeling bullied into it. I was very surprised by this one and assumed that it would mostly be held by anti-feminist men who thought that women couldn't make informed choices for themselves. But several women said this, and this feels so deeply offensive. Are adult women not able to consent? To know their own minds and be able to ask and advocate for what they want? How do they deal with the women who ask for their husbands to do this?

There is darkness and evil in domination and submission; practicing this takes you to a dark place. This argument is one that is meant well but also comes from a place of not understanding. Everything in life can take us to a dark place if we let it get out of control in our lives - be it exercise, art appreciation, work, or even cleaning your house. Certainly, taking this too far for anything will go to a dark place. But some argue that domination and submission are inherently evil, that there cannot be any power exchange without darkness and evil. I think what a lot of people mean when they say this is that they don't understand this - that it is off-putting and strange to them. There are a lot of kinks out there that I don't understand at all, so I understand that other people don't get mine at all. But not understanding a kink or being offended by it is one thing - but is there really evil in it?

Throughout the bible, there is a discussion of dominance and submission, either between people (such as a man and his wife, or between a king and his people) or between people and God, or between the parts of the Trinity. Jesus submits to God the Father to death on the Cross, even weeping and crying out against it in the garden of Gethsemane, but he submits. Paul exhorts Christians to submit to one another, for women to submit to husbands, and for slaves to obey their masters. If submission were inherently evil, why would it be all over the bible?

This is not the picture of the gentle joining of two becoming one that is written about in scripture. People who say this are usually the ones that have one idea of what marital sex should look like and were shocked when Mark Driscoll came out with a book about marriage that said that oral sex was okay.[5] It seems the wrong approach to look outside of marriage - to an authority (especially like Mark Driscoll, but I digress) as to what is righteous and what isn't. When Jesus came to earth, He didn't issue more rules; He taught core values because He knew that's what people needed. Instead of asking, "Can we ____?" (the famous second section of their book which discusses what sexual practices are okay), it's much better to ask, "Why do we?" and "How do we?" and "What is the motivation here?" and even, "How does this affect our marriage?" Every marriage is different, and what works for one couple won't work for everyone. Some couples like candles and soft music, some couples like rowdy dancing and a quickie in the back of the car, some couples like making love on different pieces of furniture around their apartment, and others like making out in the hot tub. The bible doesn't specify any type of sex as holier than the other, just that there is love, respect, and consent between the marriage partners.

If you have trouble stopping your kink, you require God's redemption in your life. This one gave me serious pause because this is the lie that held me captive for years. This is the lie that would tell me that if only I was holy enough, if I prayed enough, and if I surrendered enough to God, then I would be redeemed and transformed into what I thought I should be. But nowhere in scripture does it say that you have to earn your transformation and that God judges you worthy to become a new creation - we just are. What if we were to believe that radical idea that God has redeemed us, that He is about transforming us, and that we don't have to earn it? That He wants us to live lives of freedom, hope, and intimacy with Him that doesn't involve white-knuckling it to change our core identities first?

Reading these articles from a variety of sources, including writers who are psychologists, theologians, feminists, and bloggers, it becomes clear that most of the people writing about BDSM and Christianity don't have any idea about what it actually is and what it is for the people that identify with it. There are disgust and discomfort talking about it, and there is a definite "othering" when they talk about people who practice it. There is no understanding about it, compassion, engagement, or curiosity. If someone who had practiced BDSM at one point had decided not to practice based on religious conviction, that would be an article I would like to read - not that I would necessarily agree, but I would respect their opinion a great deal more than someone who is not at all kinky and looks down their nose at it.

What You Do with It

Acceptance of the idea of kink as an orientation doesn't mean that you then have to act on it if you aren't comfortable with it. What you do with it is entirely up to you and your faith decisions. But there is something completely different between recognizing who you are and making decisions from there and trying to deny who you are.

I'm going to break my own rule here just a little bit to talk about orientation because it is a word used a lot for people with a homosexual or a bisexual orientation. I am neither of these, but I have walked and prayed with people who have struggled with this orientation. I have known dedicated, sincere Christians with a homosexual orientation who have decided to live a celibate lifestyle based on their interpretation of scripture and their relationship with God. I have also known dedicated, sincere Christians that have joined churches that affirm their sexual orientation and have married same-sex spouses in the church. I am not going to voice an opinion here on which I think is the better choice, because I feel that this situation is up to the person's relationship with God, their convictions, and reading of scripture. However, I do think that if someone has identified as exclusively homosexual since childhood, it would be harmful to them to try and deny that orientation. I think there are people who experiment with sexuality, and that is something other than having a strong and pervasive orientation. Whatever reason that person has that particular orientation (the infamous nature versus nurture debate) isn't important because, in the end, this is a person with a pervasive identity that is very unlikely to be able to change, and will likely cause harm if you try.

The orientation doesn't change, just like your curly hair doesn't change. But it's our choice on what we do with it.

Common behaviors of young children with this kink:
- Looking up "spank" or related words in the dictionary.
- A heightened level of avoidance of disciplinary spankings, more so than their peers.
- Seeking out books and stories that describe spankings.
- Efforts to "self-spank."
- Spanking play with playmates.
- Shame and hiding around the stories that they read or write once they realize that there is something different about their kink

Chapter 2:

A Theology of Sin and Sex

I want to talk about operational theology. Don't let the word scare you, this simply means the theology that we operate under - the practical ways in which theology acts out our everyday life. Theology shouldn't be something we put on a shelf and dust off on Sundays, or when someone has a theological crisis, it is something that should permeate our everyday life. How we drive a car, how we treat our kids, how we pay our bills, and how we have sex should all be informed by our theology - which is the study of God with us.

So, based on how we have sex as a society, what do we think about sex as a society? Sex in our society right now, as we know it, is a vast array of experiences - and most of them not at all what God intended. Technology has worked to make sex more and more isolated and divorced from a relationship, with the ease of access to pornography, shallow relationships available online, etc. In reading scripture, there are a few truths that emerge when God talks about sex:

Truths About Sex:

It's about intimacy. Even the biology of how we are created speaks to this - God created us as one of the few animals that have sex outside of times when we're fertile. Most other mammals only engage in sexual activity when they're fertile, and have clear and readable signs to others of their species when they're fertile. Dogs, cats, horses, and cows go into "heat," which is a fertile period, and look to engage in sexual activity to get pregnant. Only a handful of mammals have ovulation that isn't immediately apparent, and humans are among them. For humans, not only is it nearly impossible to tell when a woman is fertile, but humans engage in sexual activity outside of times of fertility all the time - whether outside of the few days a month a woman is fertile or for the decades after forty-five when conception is unlikely. Biologically, we are created for sex that is about relationship and intimacy, not just conception.

Whenever sex goes badly in the bible, it is because it breaks this basic tenet of sex being created for intimacy - either through rape, multiple wives, outside of marriage, etc. God created sex to further intimacy in marriage through shared pleasure, vulnerability, and experience. It also often creates baby humans, but this is not its primary purpose - otherwise, people would not be encouraged to have sex when they are clearly beyond their childbearing years. And there are multiple examples in the bible of people conceiving children when they were past what was thought to be their childbearing years with no objection raised as to the lack of sexual intercourse - just the fact that they were old! So whenever the Bible talks about good sex, it always talks about the intimacy of the partners.

It's about commitment. Nowhere in scripture is healthy, God-ordained sex divorced from commitment. There is always a mutual commitment for marriage, and often (but not always), it is followed by a commitment to raise children together.

It's about consent. This one is tricky because there are a lot of places in the bible where consent isn't given, and that the bible isn't clear about this. But I think a closer reading of the bible does address this, and this is when Paul is talking to married couples about abstaining from sex. It was a practice at the time for married couples to abstain from sex, as they would often abstain from food for a short period for a specific purpose. Paul said that it was acceptable for a short time, but to not make it too long or it would be burdensome to either partner. Paul clearly states that the consent needs to be mutual; it's not even a question here.[6] And the bigger example here is how Christ treats us, as we are often told that we are the bride of Christ. God doesn't do anything to us without our consent, and our consent to the relationship is sort of the whole point. The same with sex - sex without consent is a hollow thing, a perversion, and a violent act. And consent shouldn't be just about the kind we give when we're feeling pressured, but instead the enthusiastic and willing consent of two people coming together with a great deal of love and excitement to be together. So much of the Old Testament is God longing for that enthusiastic consent from Israel, and Israel giving lukewarm and legalistic consent.

It's about mutual fulfillment. If you don't believe me, read Song of Solomon about the mutual pleasure the lovers take in their bodies and their lovemaking. Or you can go back to Paul, who very clearly says that a spouse has a responsibility to fulfill the other.[7] Or you can look at the Hebrew divorce laws - one of the reasons a woman could file for divorce from her husband according to Hebrew laws was for him not fulfilling his sexual duty to her.

So, if that's the basics about what the bible says about sex, we need to talk about what the bible says about sin. And to do this, we need to take a trip back to the beginning and look at where it began - in a garden. In that garden, when God placed the man and the woman there, there was only one sin they could commit, and that was the sin of eating the fruit from the tree of good and evil. We all know what happened - they ate the fruit, were kicked out of the garden, and discernment between good and evil from that point on became much more difficult.

Truths About Sin:

So how do we know what a sin is? Sometimes it's really easy to tell - our inner "That's not fair!" alarm goes off. Every two-year-old has a spark of the divine within them when they see a playmate getting a treat that they're denied, and they see the sin of favoritism. But you can't make a rule that says that just hurting other people is a sin because sometimes there are righteous reasons for a person to be hurt. If someone has suffered abuse for years at the hand of another person, be it friend or relative, nobody would call it a sin for them to create boundaries to keep themselves safe from further abuse, even if it hurt the abuser's feelings.

The Ten Commandments! we realize. We have rules written down! Yes, that's very true. And you have to admire their brevity to sum up all of the law, especially if you've ever been to a lawyer's office and looked at the beautifully bound books that hold the laws of our country that are decidedly longer than the Ten Commandments. But that can be hard to discern and to apply to every situation because most situations aren't remotely covered. And even the ones that are, it can still be hard! Even a simple rule such as "Don't Steal," can have a thousand different things to think about. Almost nobody believes that it's okay to walk into the store and walk out with a bunch of candy you didn't pay for, but I've heard that commandment used to defend not paying union dues, because requiring someone to pay dues to work is stealing. And then how about fair use and copyright laws? It's enough to make your head spin.

And then how about the plethora of other things that we talk about in our era that aren't even mentioned by name in the bible - like euthanasia, abortion, trade wars, colonialism, racism, feminism, racketeering, social media, sexual harassment, pedophilia, etc. Some are pretty easy to make biblical judgements about - Jesus had very harsh things to say about people hurting children, so it's safe to say he would not be happy with someone sexually molesting one of them. But others are harder to define; there are good and devout Christians on both sides arguing other social issues. So how do we decide what is sin and what isn't?

At the risk of being reductionist, I'm going to paraphrase what Jesus says that all of scripture can be boiled down to one idea: to love God and to love your neighbor. So I'm going to say that sin is anything that interferes with either loving your God or loving your neighbor well. Sin isn't the fun and naughty kid skipping class and skateboarding at the park, it's willfully separating yourself from the One that loves you the most: your Creator. Or, it's willfully separating from or hurting His creation: your fellow humans. So, therefore, sexual sin is any sexual act that separates a person from God or one another. And sin always breaks at least one of the four core principles that good sex is based on - intimacy, commitment, consent, and mutual fulfillment.

Adultery? This usually involves lying, deception, and pretty much the opposite of intimacy in a relationship, as well as breaking your commitments. Pressuring a partner for sex? Breaks consent, and also breaks down intimacy as well. Domestic Violence? This is a sin of intimacy and consent, as well as mutual fulfillment. Selfishness or Apathy? Sins of mutual fulfillment.

Is Kink a Sin?

So how does a kink like spanking fit into this discussion of marital intimacy and sin? I think it's very important to talk about it because many Christians are calling it a sin, and I disagree. But let's look at the four areas of good biblical sex and see how this kink stacks up:

Intimacy: Practicing a kink safely, with good boundaries and safe practices, can be an incredibly intimate and loving thing to do with a partner. And for a person with this kink, it is incredibly isolating to not share this with their partner. For the first fourteen years of my marriage, I didn't even hint to my husband that I had a kink. We had great sex, mind you, which I enthusiastically enjoyed, but kink-free. I longed for the intimacy to share this with him, but I dreaded the consequences of it going badly. I would ask leading questions like, "What is your sexual fantasy?" hoping that maybe he would say something that would allow me to follow up with something that I could share, but he never did. I had a fantasy that he would share that he always wanted to spank someone, and then I could follow up with my desire to be spanked, and we would be off to the races, so to speak. But it never happened, and I was left feeling alone and like a freak. I wrote stories I would never let him see, and he never pressed.

However, I became increasingly troubled by not telling my life partner and that man I trusted more than anyone else about this, and it began to leak out. He became aware that I had something to tell him, and he knew I was worried about telling him, but I just couldn't get my courage up to do it. When I was feeling it, we were taking a vacation together without the children, and he even said, "Whatever it is, maybe we can talk about it on vacation? Where we have plenty of time, and you don't have to worry about anything." I chickened out and didn't tell him on that vacation, but he was patient.

On the night I finally did tell him, several months after that vacation, I don't know why that night was different than any other night. We had gone to Costco to buy groceries, we had spent the evening joking around, and I had changed into one of my favorite negligees before slipping into bed. While touching and fondling, I was overcome with just such a deep feeling of safety, and I suddenly realized that I could tell him.

"You know when we were talking about sexual fantasies yesterday?" I asked as he kissed my neck.

"Yes," he answered.

"Well, what if I told you one of mine?"

"Sure," he answered enthusiastically. "Lay it on me."

"Well, it's a bit embarrassing," I told him. "But I've always wanted to be spanked."

"Spanked?" he answered with surprise.

"Yes," I answered, a little breathless in my daring. This was the moment - make or break. Would he reject me? Ridicule me? Tell me I was a horrible sinner? Tell our friends what a freak I was?

"Okay," he answered. "Roll over then."

"Roll over?" I answered blankly. His complete acceptance and enthusiastic participation wasn't even a response I'd envisioned.

"Maybe bending over the bed would be easier," he surmised.

I jumped to obey, my mind in complete shock. Was this happening for real, or was this just a particularly vivid fantasy I was having? Had I really just blurted out what I had spent fourteen years of marriage trying to cover up?

My first spanking from my husband was short, awkward, and completely caught me by surprise by the intensity of the reaction my body had to it. We had a lot of talking and learning to do - a LOT of talking and learning - and my very vanilla (meaning non-kinky) husband learned to understand and love his kinky wife in this way that she yearned and longed for. And, in exchange, he got a way to entice his wife into sex if she was at all feeling tired or not in the mood - he just had to do a little "dirty talk" about spanking, and she would swoon!

For me, this story is a story of intimacy. It is a story of trust, vulnerability, love, and acceptance. His reaction to my sharing my deep reality which had festered for years as deep shame led to greater intimacy and love in our marriage, and more trust than I thought possible.

Commitment: I don't see how anybody could argue that kink interferes with commitment. Again, this also has to do with how you express your kink, but within the boundaries of a loving marriage should have no problems.

Consent: This is a very large issue because, without consent, spanking, or most other practices of BDSM would be abuse. I will talk a lot more about consent in a later chapter, but suffice it to say that without consent, there should never be spanking or anything like this. And by consent, I mean enthusiastic and eager consent and ongoing consent. Every couple should have a way to stop the play immediately if either party is uncomfortable, however that works for the couple. Some couples use a safeword, or a hand signal, or simply a "that's hard enough, baby, let's take it down a notch." In BDSM, you don't consent once and then it's over; you are in a state of continual consent, and that can be withdrawn at any moment.

Mutual fulfillment: God created sex to be about mutual fulfillment, and that should be the goal of every couple, whether kinky or vanilla. I got married at the same time as several of my college friends, and one woman in this newlywed cohort used to be fond of saying, "Sex isn't done until everyone's had cookies." Nobody would argue this if what the two partners in a couple needed were different but non-kinky, but if what one person wants is kinky that's where the difficulties lie for a lot of people.

There is nothing biblically that expressly forbids kinky sex between married partners, and there's nothing implicitly evil about it either. God wants sex between married partners to be hot, exciting, nurturing, sacred, fulfilling, bonding, and fun. The people that speak out against kinky sex do so out of a personal revulsion or misunderstanding of kink and sexual diversity, not out of biblical authority. But if the bible doesn't have a problem with kinky sex, what about psychology?

Chapter 3:

Kink and Psychology

To begin with, in writing this chapter, I would like to say that I am a licensed, masters-level psychotherapist that is currently practicing in private practice. I am not a sex therapist, nor is sex therapy a large part of my practice. I do, however, work with many people who have been the victims of sexual abuse, domestic violence, and rape. I want you to know what I do professionally to know my expertise and to also know my limitations; some people study this topic exclusively and dedicate their lives to research. I am not one of those people, but I would like to talk a little bit about the history of BDSM, Psychology, and what it means to us today.

Sigmund Freud, often called the father of psychiatry, had a lot of views on sex, and many of them remain controversial even today. But he was also the first one to quantify what was a sexual perversion, and he fell squarely in the camp of any type of BDSM was a sexual perversion, and one that needs to be "cured." This should not be surprising, as psychiatry at the time was a product of the Victorian culture, and it thought that anything other than penile-vaginal sex was aberrant. The DSM, which is the source for diagnosing mental illnesses, listed homosexuality as a mental illness until the early 1970s.

Kink as a Paraphilia

The DSM still currently pathologizes BDSM, listing it as a "paraphilia (302.83, 302.84)" and defining it as having "sexual fantasies, urges or behaviors which involve inflicting (or having inflicted on oneself) psychological or physical suffering to enhance or achieve sexual excitement." There are caveats, however, in that it has to have lasted at least six months and has to have caused distress or difficulty in interpersonal or occupational functioning.[8] Before the release of the DSM-5 in 2013, any interest in BDSM was diagnosable, but the DSM-5 made distress a requirement. So, while this is an improvement, this diagnosis is troubling for several reasons.

First, this classification puts BDSM lumped together with other paraphilias that are non-consensual and often criminal, such as pedophilia, voyeurism, and frotteurism. Comparing loving, consensual kink within a committed relationship seems like an incredibly different thing than a lonely, broken person trying to peek in windows or setting up cameras for sexual pleasure. Secondly, this classification also assumes that people with the orientation towards BDSM are unhappy, and this adds to their pathology, and researchers that have undertaken the study of this have been shocked to find out that this isn't the case. Researchers found that practitioners of BDSM were more psychologically healthy than a control group by most measures, and reported lower levels of anxiety and depression.[9]

What if the distress that can accompany BDSM results not from the BDSM itself but from the pressure from the surrounding community and indeed even the psychological community itself? When talking about the DSM diagnosis and BDSM, one researcher writes, "Also, because of the taboos around BDSM in our culture, being involved in BDSM may well involve 'significant distress or impairment in...functioning' for a time, precisely because of the stigma, social unacceptability, discrimination, and prejudice surrounding it."[10]

What if the distress, shame and difficulty surrounding BDSM identities could be alleviated not by attempting to "cure" people with these fantasies and urges, but instead letting them accept themselves for who they were and love themselves for the orientation they had? What if a BDSM orientation was as normalized as having blonde hair or an interest in high-adrenaline sports? And lastly, for something to be pathology, it should also not affect the majority of the population. Studies have found that a majority of the population has at least one BDSM-related fantasy, and about half the population has had at least one BDSM-related experience in real life.[11] It's hard to argue something is pathology if it is as prevalent as that.

The other important thing to distinguish when talking about BDSM and psychology is about how consent enters into the conversation. When talking about BDSM, it is important to distinguish between safe and consensual practices between adults versus a person who seeks sexual sadism as a non-consensual act. These two things are as different as loving consensual lovemaking and rape, yet sometimes they are not differentiated between very well.[12] Some researchers and theorists are finding that the inclusion of BDSM in the DSM only makes sense continuingly as a forensic diagnosis for non-consensual encounters,[13] which makes it more like the other paraphilias it's classified with. I agree with this; I think

BDSM should only be in the DSM for non-consensual sexual sadism.

Kink in the Therapy Office

Psychology has had a long and difficult history with kinky people, with one researcher finding 118 out of 175 BDSM clients reporting "biased or inadequate" care from their psychotherapists.[14] In all honesty, even though I have been in therapy on and off for years, I have never talked about my kink with my therapist either, and a big part of that was because I was a therapist that was trained at the same graduate school as my therapist, and I likely could predict how she would handle my kink. My graduate school is Christian, but progressively so.

At my graduate school (where I was in training to become a psychotherapist), we read a book about marital sex and it included a story about a client mentioning that she liked sex with her new husband (both she and her new husband had lost their first spouses) much more than with her first husband, partially because her new husband would often give her a little spanking before sexual encounters with him. I was thrilled when I read this in the required reading - were we going to have a spanking-positive discussion about sex and kinkiness? This was before I had "come out" to my husband, and I longed for some affirmation that I was normal or okay. I eagerly awaited my next class, hoping to get some answers. Alas, answers I didn't get - instead, my professor (who was the president of the school at the time) laughed a bit when someone asked him about the book. He said that he couldn't endorse everything in the book. Then he said something that struck my heart - he said that sexual fantasy hurts relationships. He went on to say that games, role-playing, and fantasies all detracted from the connection sex was supposed to form, with some side remarks on how shameful it was that the number one selling costume for women to dress up in was a schoolgirl outfit - an obvious outlet for barely disguised pedophilia.

I was heartsick; could this be true? Could even my most innocent of fantasies - I often fantasized of my husband and me alone in a rustic cabin or on the beach when we were making love - be bad? And could a schoolgirl outfit, which I saw as an outplaying of one of my favorite fantasies, really just be a cover for pedophilia?

I look back now at the professor and have a lot of grace for him, and realize that he was reacting more from what he saw as an over-sexualization of children, a reaction to the countless children and adults he has treated for childhood sexual abuse. He sees that because he is most likely thoroughly vanilla; he's not thinking about kink. If he had realized how invested somebody might be in the fantasy of sex and how much it impacted their identity, he would never have made so light of it. I doubt it occurred to him that I was sitting in the class, looking thoroughly respectable, secretly longing for someone to assure me that my desire to be spanked didn't mean that I was sick, twisted, and beyond redemption.

When I have worked with kinky clients, I have watched them hedge and test me a bit before they come out to me. I tested my therapist in the same way, and it was easy to tell that she was not going to be welcoming to my kinky side. I don't think she would have been condemning, but I needed a therapist that wasn't just going to be neutral, but understanding. She would have seen it as a symptom and tried to find a trauma that caused it and not understand it as a part of my orientation. Other schools may have more thorough training, but I have never heard of a therapist that is adequately trained on how to address BDSM clients. Many rely on outdated and popular culture tropes, which are perpetuated in everything from *50 Shades of Grey* to *A Dangerous Method* about how BDSM is simply reenacting abuse from one's childhood, which has not been substantiated by research.

The problem is, there is work that needs to be done with kinky clients around their kink and relationships. One kinky client I worked with didn't test me for too long before seeing how I would react to her kink - and I think part of that was due to her desperation for help in dealing with it. Her partner in kink was someone who was treating her badly and not staying within the kink guidelines, pushing her farther than she felt comfortable and disrespecting the limits she set. When I didn't condemn her for the kink she enjoyed and was actually able to use the right lingo, saying, "Isn't it considered unethical of him to push your hard limits like that?" and "How does he respond to your safeword?" She was able to process what about the relationship wasn't working, what she wanted in a relationship, and was able to break it off with him. And that is consistent with what research has found: Most kinky people, when they go to therapy, aren't there for therapy about their kink - they're there for relational therapy, but having a therapist that is culturally competent in their kink is helpful.[15]

The American Psychological Association (APA) has put out guidelines for working with the LGBTQ community for mental health practitioners, but they have been much quieter about the BDSM community (though to be fair, they do have a few articles on "sex positivity," which covers BDSM). The guidelines that they put out for working with the LGBTQ community could easily be the same and applied to the kink community with very little translation. But for now, here's my take on some good guidelines for mental health practitioners and consumers around BDSM:

1. Kink is not a mental illness.
2. Kink is a normal variant of human sexuality and trying to change it is likely futile and could cause harm.
3. Kink is not caused by trauma, but sometimes kinky people use their kink to help them process their

trauma. Just like being a writer or an artist isn't caused by trauma, but people use their art to process their trauma.

4. Practitioners of kink face a great deal of discrimination in the community and their families, and often have a great deal of internal shame.

5. Therapists should think about how their own attitudes towards kink might affect their ability to be effective and refer as necessary.

6. Therapists should recognize that there is a wide variety of experiences and desires within the kink community.

Chapter 4:

What About Feminism?

I'm a feminist, even though my in-laws think it's a bad word. If you are not a feminist and you object to reading about feminism, then feel free to skip this chapter in its entirety; it won't hurt my feelings. But, for those who stayed, I want to say that it continues to amaze me why it seems like such a radical idea that women are co-heirs and created equal partners to their mates. And just like the policy of "separate but equal" was not real equality in education between the races in twentieth-century America, real equality doesn't come by putting one gender in power and in charge of the other. If you disagree with me theologically, that's completely fine. The point of this book isn't the apologetics that are going to convince anybody of that idea, but rather the implications of that theory. If you believe in equality with the sexes, there are some implications to people with this kink.

BDSM as Ritualized Violence Against Women

There is a train of thought that BDSM practices victimize women and are external manifestations of the sexist power structure, and this line of thought is particularly aimed at women who take the submissive role in BDSM play. People who believe this think that women who consent to BDSM activities can't really consent because they are within a sexist power structure, and they say that if women were free to choose regardless of the power structure, then they would choose less submissive interactions. Some even go so far as to say that women are fooled into eroticizing their pain.[16]

To be honest, as a person that has had this kink my whole life, I feel so patronized by this view that I have a very hard time taking it seriously. This has to be written by people who have no view of BDSM as an orientation, or for women as sentient, independent people that can make their own decisions. I feel far more infantilized by academics saying that I have no agency in making decisions about my sexual identity than I do by asking my husband for what I want sexually and him fulfilling those desires.

I can certainly imagine scenarios where women are victimized by BDSM, just like they are victimized by regular sexual activity every day. There are perpetrators that practice BDSM just like there are perpetrators that are gay, straight, Democrats, Republicans, rich, poor, and a lot of other things. But victimizing someone using BDSM against their consent is a crime, and should be reported to the police and prosecuted as assault.

I see this as very similar to the argument that some feminists make against women who want to be stay-at-home mothers. This branch says that for women to take this role, this role is giving in to the patriarchy that has oppressed women for centuries and that if women were free to choose, they would choose careers and live much like men have done. The problem with this chain of thought is that there are women who want to stay home and be housewives, and trying to make them feel like bad feminists for wanting to do so is actually anti-feminist. True feminism is allowing each woman to decide what works for her and her family, whether it's her staying home, both parents working, or her husband staying home.

Likewise, true feminism should recognize women as autonomous, intelligent beings that recognize their nature and needs in relationships and with their sexuality.

Feminism and the Sex-Positive Movement

In recent years, more modern feminists have taken a more sex-positive stance about BDSM and see it as a sexual expression that can be consistent with feminism. This view sees BDSM as a sexual orientation or an ethical option, and therefore not inconsistent with an ethical expression of feminism.[17] This is a much better recognition of BDSM as a positive activity rather than simply men oppressing women, and also is recognizing that men often choose to be the submissive partners in BDSM relationships.

Another argument that sex-positive feminist thinkers make is that over-regulation and criticism of a woman's sex life is an extension of the patriarchy because its academics, legislators, and others thinking they have the authority to regulate and criticize women's sexual expression.[18] And I think this speaks to the part of feminism that should be about respecting women's autonomy and intelligence - any attempt to wrest control of these things from women is anti-feminist.

Feminism and Ethical Expression

This is the part of the feminist conversation where every person has to decide their ethical considerations for themselves. Nobody should do anything in their BDSM practices that go against their ethics in the real world. In the world of fantasy, I think it's a different story, as in the world of fantasy, we can explore those with nobody getting hurt. Let me explain.

Before I told my husband about my fantasies and started practicing my orientation in real life, I had a rich world of fantasies, both in my writing and in my head. One of my favorite fantasies was around punishment - the stern, loving husband/father/teacher person delivering a well-deserved, stern but fair spanking on a miscreant's backside. If the miscreant was a child, the scenario felt not at all sexual. If the miscreant was a grown woman, and the spanker was her husband, I would often have some fluttering of sexual feelings in my fantasy.

But then came reality, and it made me realize how different fantasy was from reality. I quickly realized how much this scenario that I was dreaming and writing about differed from my feminist ethics; there was no way that I was going to ever be comfortable with my husband having this sort of power over me. My husband recognized it first, actually, when I was describing my fantasies to him.

"I get that this is part of your fantasy," he told me. "But I don't see how this is going to work. I just can't think of a scenario where it would be okay for me to actually punish you."

And he was right, there wasn't a scenario. It offended my deep sense of our relationship, our purpose, and the belief that God created us to be equal partners in life together. Having my husband punish me for something, even though it felt really attractive in my fantasy life, wasn't something that I wanted in real life.

But what was I to do with these fantasies that I had? It was so hot to have my husband tell me I was naughty and that he was going to take me over his knee later that night; I didn't want to give that feeling up. So my husband and I sought a compromise, which is a compromise many married couples seek when one (or both) spouses want something else that is unethical in and of itself. When a spouse fantasizes about picking up a stranger in a bar to have sex with them, what if the person they pick up is their spouse? If the fantasy is that the pizza man/boss and secretary/or whatever scenario happens, instead of having extramarital sex, you can play-act it with your spouse. So we did not set up that he would punish me in real life, but we could act like he was doing it. He could simply tell me I was naughty, or we could even invent a scenario complete with costumes (depending on the time and mood).

Whatever you find, your ethical expression of your kink needs to be something you approach with a lot of thought and prayer. Not every fantasy and kink is going to have an ethical expression in the real world, but if it aligns with your ethical standards, then don't let the patriarchy tell you differently!

Chapter 5:

Why Are You Kinky?

If you came to this chapter hoping for a definitive answer as to why you are the way you are, I want to start by saying that you probably are not going to like the answer. This answer often bothers people, and it bothers people that write kink so much that many common tropes and misconceptions have entered common mainstream thinking. I'm going to address those, and show how they are wrong, at least in my own experience and those of many kinksters I know. That's not to say that they're wrong for everybody; it's completely possible that there is a person that craves spankings because of unresolved guilt or that they are re-enacting a traumatic childhood, but that is not the norm.

I also want to differentiate that there is an interest in kink that lies on a spectrum, just like with anyone else. Some people might have a passing interest in getting a swat or two from a boyfriend in college, and some people identify this as a core part of their identity. This chapter is more about people who see this as a core part of their identity, not something that might be fun to try once or twice.

Sigmund Freud and Childhood Spanking

It always seems proper to start with ol' Siggy. Freud theorized that people who crave spankings were stuck in immature sexuality, from when the entire body experienced sexualized feelings. Therefore, sometimes, when a parent spanked a child, the child experienced arousal, and then this arousal became tied to the spanking. People (he usually meant women) who never moved past this stayed in a state of immature sexuality, and that treatment with him or one of his doctors could cure them. The problem with this line of thought is that many people have this kink that wasn't spanked as children. I was spanked a few times as a child, but I found it distressing and not at all arousing. I studiously avoided being spanked as a child, despite my rich fantasy life about it. Researchers have found no difference between people who are spanked as children or not spanked as children in whether or not they are kinky.[19]

I want to start this section by saying that I come from a small, rural town, and I grew up in the 1970s and early 80s, so spanking was considered a completely normal consequence in most families. In fact, public schools had spanking in them until I was in middle school. My fifth-grade teacher had a paddle that he would sometimes utilize for specific infractions, and the recipient would always have the option after their correction to sign the paddle as a mark of their bravery. At the end of the year, the teacher said that he wanted to give any kid that hadn't had a chance to sign the paddle the chance to do it - but the price was taking a swat from the paddle in front of the class.

Several kids took him up on the offer, and I sat in my chair completely glued to it - barely believing the spectacle I was witnessing. But there was another truth that I knew to my very bones; I was not going to volunteer. This may sound odd, as I spent so much of my fantasy life longing and yearning for a spanking that I wouldn't take my opportunity when I had a socially sanctioned option for one, but there was no way I was going to do this. Spankings didn't mean to me what they meant to other kids - for me, they were something very personal and intense. It wasn't just a smack and a sting on my bottom; this was something very different.

It Must Be Trauma

Trauma is a buzzword right now; it is all the rage in the psychological world, and for very good reasons. With the recognition of how much Adverse Childhood Experiences (ACEs) affect everything from addiction to pancreatic cancer, scientists are rushing to figure out how to help people with the single most life-shortening factor that they've found yet. Researchers compiled a list of ten common childhood traumas and found that people who have at least five of them die an average of twenty years sooner than people who have less than five of them.[20] I am a trauma therapist, and I take this very seriously, and I see this every day in the work that I do. So trust me when I say that this is not how trauma works.

When you have Post Traumatic Stress Disorder (PTSD), one of the diagnostic criteria is that you avoid whatever is triggering the trauma. When a soldier comes back from a war, they will often avoid fireworks or other things that sound like war or smell like war. People that associate yelling with abuse will go to great lengths to avoid people that yell. People that have been bitten by a dog as a young child will often avoid dogs at all costs, even small and harmless ones. Soldiers have flashbacks to war that they find disturbing and upsetting, not erotic. A person bitten by a dog doesn't have erotic fantasies about playing Frisbee with a dog; they have nightmares about being chased by one. PTSD wouldn't cause people to be attracted to things like spankings; it would make them avoid them. Kinky people with a history of childhood abuse can wonder why they are attracted to spankings when physical abuse was such a source of pain in their childhood, but science seems to say that they are attracted to spankings not because of their trauma but despite their trauma.

Psychology has also found no link between childhood trauma and kink. Practitioners of BDSM are about as psychologically healthy if not more so than the general population.[21] But there are a lot of stories of people working through their trauma using their kink, including from some of my clients. But I think this is the difference between causality and psychiatric health; kinky people will use their kink to help keep them healthy. For instance, I am a writer and have been since I could start putting words into sentences. So whenever anything traumatic happens to me, I feel that I can't process it properly until I write about it. I think for some people, kink can be that processing for them, that way of embodying and getting control of what happened to them. I don't think that the trauma caused their kink any more than I think my trauma caused me to become a writer, but people use their tools of creativity and expression to make their world make sense.

When I work with children that have had trauma, I always play with them with dolls, art, Legos, sand tray, and dart guns and anything else that is a creative space. Usually, when they feel safe enough, they will eventually get around to playing out the dynamics of the trauma in our play together. This is good and necessary for them to be able to feel mastery of what happened to them, for them to feel the power in the situation, for them to move the story from their subconscious to their conscious, and for them to grieve. Sometimes this reenactment takes a few sessions; sometimes it takes months. But kids do it as much as they need to do it, and then they move on. When I read accounts of people re-enacting their trauma with their kink, I get the same feeling as I do when I work with children with trauma. Yes, this play space is sacred, and yes, I think this is important work that they are doing with their partner in this play space. The mastery they are finding over their story, the power they are feeling, moving the story from the subconscious to the conscious, and the grieving is all incredibly good. But I think for most of the people that are doing this that this is using a pre-existing kink for a good purpose, but it didn't cause the kink.

Because Science

My undergraduate degree was in hard science, and I have spent some time before psychology in the hard science and medical world. It was very tempting in the world of biology to reduce every human impulse down to a desire to reproduce. My biology professor in undergraduate told us that the meaning of life was "to produce successful offspring, so our genes survive," and that everything we did was to that end purpose.

Do you like men with broad shoulders? Good providers for your offspring. Do men like women with shapely curves? Good childbearing hips. You're trying to do well in college to secure future employment? You're trying to provide for said offspring. You can see how reductionist and defeatist it can feel very quickly. Even having a good emotional bond with your partner can be seen as biologically advantageous for the care of the offspring. The problem is that all these things are true - secondary sexual characteristics do tend to attract mates better, and a good emotional bond with your mate does make caring for offspring better. However, humans all over the world can agree that the truth to what the meaning of life truly happens to be is far more complex than just a sum of our genes surviving. If it was just a matter of our genes surviving, would people adopt? Is art created just to hoodwink people into mating with us? And once our offspring are successfully producing offspring of their own, are we useless?

I say this because many people see spanking and other BDSM practices purely as biological and medical. They talk about the endorphins, nerve endings, and such, which are all true. Spanking does release endorphins that are similar to a runner's high, and the nerve endings that are activated during a spanking can feel good and can often wake up the clitoris and all sorts of fun areas of the body. The bottom is an erogenous zone, but the nerve endings are deep and under a layer of fat and muscle - which requires a deep way of activating those nerve endings.

But for a lot of people, it was the psychological craving that happened for YEARS before the physical part of it was fulfilled. I was truly shocked by how sexual spanking was for me, and I am not alone in that discovery. If science was truly the cause of my kink, then I would have accidentally stumbled upon it, realized that these nerve endings were stimulated in this way, and then gone about finding ways to stimulate them. If biology was the key to this, then there wouldn't be all the trappings that go along with it as well - the ambiance, the costumes, the stories. We are far more complex creatures than just our biology, and our sexuality is far more complex than reducing it down to brain chemicals and nerve endings. Yes, those chemicals and nerve endings are important to our experience of sex. No, they are not the whole story.

Guilt

Some people think that people attracted to spanking are trying to work through unresolved guilt from their childhood. In some ways, this is Christian Grey, main BDSM practitioner of *Fifty Shades of Grey*, the book that propelled spanking and BDSM into popular culture by completely misrepresenting it hugely. He is pretty clear and self-reflective in an incredibly shallow way that he likes to have submissives that look like his heroin-addicted mom, so he can alternate between controlling and caring for them by dictating proper exercise and food, and then by spanking them. If I had a client doing this behavior, I wouldn't think healthy BDSM behavior; I would be thinking about guilt and shame from unresolved childhood trauma.

Studies have also shown that people who practice BDSM are not measurably more neurotic, which you would expect that people who would be suffering from guilt would be. Practitioners of BDSM though, do score higher on conscientiousness, meaning that they like order and rules and tend to be more honest and humble.[22] It could be that this conscientiousness does add to the desire for order, and part of that order is punishment, but I think that's missing an entire aspect of this kink. Would someone with this kink be happy with being grounded instead of spanking? Do people fantasize about having a financial penalty for doing something they know to be outside of their ethics? Not likely. If wanting to be spanked were caused by unresolved guilt from your childhood, wouldn't your desire to be spanked resolve once you were spanked? Wouldn't the spanking itself lean more towards relief and catharsis rather than erotic fun?

I'm not saying that guilt isn't a factor and the fact that people that like spanking tend to be very conscientious is certainly a sign that that might be a factor. But it can't be the only factor, and it can't be the cause.

Mental Illness

This illness model of mental health can be really helpful when talking about something like bipolar or depression. With either of these conditions, the person has measurable problems, medication, and/or therapy brings them to a condition of pre-diagnosis health (or at least better health), and the person goes on to lead a relatively normal life. Okay, this is a massive oversimplification and outrageously discounts the suffering of people with real mental illness, but I'm referring to the illness model of mental health, and how it can be really helpful for certain conditions. And using it to describe practitioners of BDSM is an enormous misstep.

There are all sorts of disorders that were once diagnosed but are no longer so. The most famous of which is probably homosexuality. Medical science no longer considers homosexuality a diagnosable condition, and the DSM-V only considers BDSM a diagnosable condition if it causes distress to the practitioner.

If BDSM is an illness, it is a congenital disability rather than an acquired birth defect. Spanking is something that is deeply embedded in people's psyches and often exists as some of their earliest memories. Some people come by it a bit later, but often it happens before or around puberty. And it is usually not something that goes away by wishing, by therapy, or by medications.

Kink as an Orientation

So what does it mean that kink is an orientation then? It means that it is a part of who you are, and so much so that it's not something you can change, nor should you try. I spent years asking why! Going between the different answers, and finding that none satisfied. I knew deeply that none of the answers I tried on was really the reason I had my kink, but sometimes I could convince myself for a short time. It always felt less shameful if there was a logical reason for my kink, especially if it felt like there was a reason I could satisfy, and maybe it could go away. Shame was the great motivator for my "why?" question - I just wanted to feel normal.

And then, I found myself doing an exercise that therapists often do with adults that were sexually abused as children, and that's to picture themselves as children the age that they were when they were abused. I have clear memories of being in first grade and being attracted to spankings in stories I read, so I thought of one of my daughters who was in first grade at the time. If she came to me and told me that she was having this issue, would I condemn her? Would I blame her and shame her for what was going on in her brain? Or would I give her grace and understanding? Looking at the innocent eyes of my child at that age, I realized that if she were having the same thoughts that I was having at that age, I wouldn't be concerned with the why - because I would attribute it to either just how she was made or in response to something that happened when she was so young that it didn't really matter. What if I gave myself the same grace that I would give my daughter?

Chapter 6:

Making Friends with Your Kink

The statistics change from study to study, but they usually show around one-third of people report fantasies around spanking. Women tend to fantasize about being spanked slightly more often, and men tend to fantasize about doing the spanking a bit more, but it ends up being one of the most common sexual fantasies, and especially one of the most common ones that fit under the banner of BDSM.[23] And it has been around forever; they have found frescoes from fifth century BC in Italy depicting erotic flogging, and the Kama Sutra lists four hand positions for the spanker, and six positions for the person receiving the spanking.[24] So an interest in spanking is a cross-cultural, cross-generational orientation that people have been trying to figure out for a very long time.

I work with people that have conditions such as Autism, ADHD, Anxiety, Phobias, PTSD, and so on. One of the things that can be very helpful for people with these types of diagnosis is to begin to find ways to make peace with their diagnosis, and even better if they can make friends with it. For instance, this is what it can look like for a teenager with ADHD: They come into therapy hating their diagnosis, feeling different, and hating that they have to take meds and are different from their neurotypical peers. Through therapy, we talk about their diagnosis and being neuro-atypical, and help normalize it as something that isn't unusual. Sometimes clients can even find something positive about their diagnosis, such as a teen with ADHD's ability to go all day without getting tired. People can often get to a place of accepting their differences through education - learning what the differences are and what they mean - by normalizing their differences - seeing that others have the same differences - and by seeing how those differences make them uniquely them.

This is not an easy thing to do, and it has been a journey for me, and a journey that I'm still on. So what does it mean to make friends with your kink? You mostly already know how if you know how to make a friend. Here's what we learned as children on how to make friends:

You get to know a friend. You should take time to get to know more about your kink, and there's a lot to learn about. Think about your kink as something to be curious about rather than something to condemn. How does that shift it for you? Once I told my husband about my kink, I suddenly went from trying to suppress my kink to wanting to learn about it. I think that this is not an accident - the acceptance I felt from my husband influenced my ability to befriend my kink just a little bit. I spent the next several months learning everything I could, no longer avoiding my kink in hopes that it would go away.

You set limits on friends. Healthy friendships have limits for time, emotional availability, drama, and safety. If your kink is causing you to meet with unknown people in unsafe places, it is time for some limits. If it is taking the time that you should be spending doing things like work or connecting with people in real life, then that also should spark a need for limits. Just like if you have a friend that you like but wants to spend every evening with you, you gently give them limits and work out a schedule that works for everyone.

Friends recognize flaws, but also appreciate the good things about the other. Before making friends with my kind, I focused entirely on the guilt and shame and didn't think of any of the good things at all. I still sometimes get sucked into feeling shame, but I also recognize the fun and the enjoyment I get from my kink as well. My kink has provided a lot of fun between my husband and me, including date nights and nights away, as well as hot, exciting quickies. I appreciate what my friend has given to me.

I am kind to my friends. I don't shame, blame, and mistreat my friends; I recognize their humanity and treat them with kindness. I realize this is a bit of a stretch because your kink is not a person, but it is a good idea to think about how to treat this part of yourself with kindness. Because if kink truly is a part of your identity, then mistreating your kink is mistreating yourself, and many people have already done enough of that to last a lifetime.

We are wise about to whom we make introductions. This gets a little bit more complicated, but let me put it like this: I do have friends in my real life that I never introduce to each other because I know that they will drive each other crazy. Likewise, I am writing this book under a pen name because there are many people in my church, my clients at my practice, my children, and other parents at my kid's soccer team that do not need to know this much about my sex life. There are a few friends I've alluded to a few of these issues, but the only person I've been completely honest with is my husband. I think it is wise to be on the conservative end of things with disclosure because it is not something you can take back. And if you are a younger person that hasn't had kids yet, it might be a good idea to think about how disclosures might feel if you eventually have children. Some people are far more open than me, and that's completely fine, just make sure you are wise and choosing trustworthy people to trust with your secrets. Unfortunately, people with this sexual orientation suffer from a host of discriminations upon disclosure, including from the medical field, psychiatric field, friends, colleagues, and in divorce or child custody cases.[25]

You enjoy, cherish, and value friends. Most of all, friends are there to enrich your lives. You don't have friends that you don't cherish and value; people you don't enjoy aren't friends - they're either a neighbor, a relative, or you feel a call from God to help them. Friends are people that you welcome in a reciprocal relationship, people that you welcome and enjoy, people that you love.

The Genie in the Bottle

At the beginning of my book, I said that if I found a genie in a bottle in my first forty years, one of my first wishes would have been for the genie to take away my desire to be spanked. This is a device that therapists often use to help a client talk about how they would like their lives to be different, and to help them envision how things could be different. Now, this is how I envision this conversation going:

"I am the Genie of the lamp! You get three wishes!"

"Great!" I answer. "That's amazing!"

"You can't wish for more wishes," the Genie tells me. "And all the standard things apply like you can't bring people back from the dead or make anyone fall in love with you. But otherwise, you're all good. What do you want?"

"How about ending world hunger?" I ask. "I wish for enough healthy food for everyone!"

"Done!" the Genie answers. "What next?"

"I want to reduce global warming and leave a healthy, functional world for our children."

"Done!" the Genie answers. "But for your third wish, policy says you have to do something personally for yourself. Isn't there something you want for yourself?"

"Funny, you should ask," I tell him. "Ten years ago, I would have asked you to get rid of something about me, but now I'm not so sure."

"Well, what benefit does it give you?" the Genie asks.

"It has certainly spiced up my sex life," I answered. "I have been enjoying that part of it a lot."

"And what does it cost you?" the Genie presses.

"Not as much as it once did," I admit. "It used to cost me a lot in guilt and shame, as well as fear and wondering what would happen if my husband found out. Well, I told him, and he took it well. He was fine with it, and he even spanks me like I've wanted all along. It's pretty amazing."

"So do you want it gone or not?" the Genie asks.

"Well, I've sort of made friends with it," I explain. "I don't think I want it gone at all. It's different now; I've been having fun with it. Nope, I think if I change anything about myself, maybe I'll make myself thinner or give me a billion dollars. That sounds way better."

Chapter 7:
Pop Culture Myths

This might shock you, but the seminal book about BDSM, the book that brought it out of the shadows of the naughty bookstores and onto the kindles of the American housewives, I hate. Yes, I'm talking about *Fifty Shades of Grey* by EL James,[26] quite possibly one of the worst representations of BDSM I've read. I think that the reason people like it so much is the reason that I like the movie *Cutthroat Island* - I like pirate movies, so any pirate movie I'm going to like, even one as bad as that one. People like books about sex, especially naughty ones, and this book just happened to capture people's imaginations at the right time, and it became a socially accepted way to consume softcore porn. I also think that there are a lot of people out there with a secret attraction to spanking that they would rather admit to being attracted to "hot" sex than to spanking. But this book has some major flaws and perpetuates most of the myths rampant in popular culture.

Myth 1: Consent Is Merely a Yes

In full disclosure, I have not read all of this book. I just couldn't get past the bad writing and the complete disregard for the main character's personhood, and it offended my feminist self so much that I couldn't read it. Perhaps it was so much better in the second half that it made up for the inadequacies of the first half, but I somehow doubt it. Consent was at the heart of the problem with this book, even though the book tried to pay lip-service to consent with the idea of the contract.

What does consent mean? Sexual consent is a hot-button topic right now in the world; college campuses are having training on what it means, and it's at the heart of the "me too" movement and the increasing awareness around issues of sexual assault. Consent in sexual situations doesn't simply mean the lack of protest to a certain behavior; it means enthusiastic agreement and a joining together for mutual pleasure. When one person is manipulated or coerced into giving their consent, they end up feeling used. This is the opposite goal of the intimacy that sex is supposed to result in; instead, it creates space and shame.

In the book *50 Shades of Grey*, the two main characters dance around the subject of consent. During this dance, Christian Grey takes all sorts of liberties in his relationship with Anastasia, including things such as selling her car (and replacing it with a new one) and "protecting" her several times when she was in no real danger. Christian is trying to get Ana to become his full-time submissive partner, and for her to sign a contract to this effect. Ana, a completely naive and irresistible young woman just finishing college, has to research to figure out what most of the contract Christian proposes even means. But instead of giving her time, patience, and education as well as a gentle introduction into what this kink might entail, he pressures her, crosses the boundaries she sets for him, and acts with ownership and jealousy towards her before any agreement has been reached.

Proper consent is something that is entered into fully knowing what you agree to, you enthusiastically agree to it, and consent is ongoing. For instance, let's say a married couple discusses trying oral sex for the first time. They are both nervous, but talk about their nerves, and maybe negotiate terms (such as pre-encounter showers). They set a date, and the encounter begins just fine. But, let's say during the encounter, the husband suddenly just starts feeling as if this isn't working for him, and he's not enjoying it. He shouldn't have to continue because this is something they've agreed to do, his consent can be withdrawn at any time in the encounter. Of course, for a healthy couple, there should be follow-up and discussion on why he was uncomfortable, but until or if ever he feels comfortable doing this with her, he should not feel pressured to give his consent.

Proper consent always:
1. Is given enthusiastically.
2. Is done by mutual agreement.
3. Can be withdrawn at any time.

Myth 2: Kink Always Comes from Damage

The story *50 Shades of Grey* also perpetuates this myth, as Christian Grey comes from a very troubled background of early childhood trauma with whom he describes as his "crack whore mother" who died in front of him. He is also the victim of sexual abuse as a teenager as a family friend introduces him to BDSM and teaches him the -er- "ropes" of the kink. He never has a "vanilla" (non-BDSM) sexual encounter until he meets Ana.

Myth 3: Kink Can Be "Cured"

In *50 Shades of Grey*, Christian loves Ana, and Ana doesn't love kink, so Christian has to learn how to be "cured" - or how to become vanilla. This myth flows straight from Myth #2 because if it is a symptom of damage, then of course, it can be cured. The entire plot of *50 Shades of Grey* seems to be how they will sort out this kink thing between them - will Ana embrace it? Will Christian be "cured?"

Myth #4 Kink Always Involves Sex

In reality, kink often involves sex, but it doesn't always. I think a part of the origin of this myth is that anything that evokes such passion and emotion has to involve sex for people. You see this in popular culture from *50 Shades of Grey* to nearly every other depiction of BDSM I've ever seen in popular culture. But the truth is that in most BDSM groups, clubs, and gatherings, sex is not allowed, and often the services of professional dominants and submissives don't involve sex.

Myth #5 BDSM Is the Same as Sexual Sadism

There is a difference between BDSM and sexual sadism and masochism, which involves the physical or psychological suffering to one's partner or oneself, and is often criminal. BDSM, in contrast, involves the role-playing and consensual playing out of similar acts in a safe and sane way - not by actually making the other person suffer.[27] A real practitioner of BDSM would never want to "play" with another partner unless the other partner was into it and enjoying it, unlike what happens when Christian spanks Ana for the first time - which she finds painful and traumatizing. Someone with sexual sadism doesn't care about consent and enjoys watching someone suffer.

Myth #6 All Kinks are Pretty Similar

I think of this as the "everyone in leather" phenomenon. Have you ever noticed that if anybody in pop culture wants to signal kink, they dress someone up in leather and give them a crop? I find this a little laughable because I don't find leather sexy at all; I find it rather off-putting. Kink has an extremely wide variety, and what fits under the BDSM umbrella is anything that wants to fit under the BDSM umbrella. There are so many things that I would never have thought would be sexy to someone that is sexy to someone that I can't even name them all; let's let say kink comes in a wondrous variety.

Myth #7 You Can Tell Who's into Kink

In almost any movie that shows a character that's into kink, they have hair dyed a crazy color, piercings, and leather clothes. I guarantee you that if you knew me in real life, you would have no idea I was into kinky stuff. I come across as very straight-laced and conservative, maybe a little bit of a Christian hippie.

Chapter 8:

Unhealthy Kink

There are unhealthy kinks, just like there are unhealthy eating and unhealthy sex. Anything in our lives that is a source of pleasure is fraught with the possibility of abuse, whether it is extreme sports or Netflix binging. I want to approach this carefully because people usually have so much built-in shame around this issue already, and I don't want to add to it, but I think it's important to talk about healthy and righteous expressions of this kink versus unhealthy ones. I don't want to give a long list of acceptable dos and don'ts; I don't think that's helpful, because what might be healthy for one person isn't healthy for another. So instead, I'm going to give general outlines and some examples of how these have applied in my own life.

Our bodies have all sorts of appetites for things - relationships, exercise, entertainment, chocolate - and that is completely normal and how we're built. But for every appetite, there are righteous and unrighteous expressions of that appetite. For instance, I like chocolate. There are righteous expressions for this appetite - perhaps a nice piece or two of chocolate after dinner, maybe a shared chocolate dessert with my friend, or some chocolate flavoring in a protein bar I'm eating for a snack. But there are unrighteous expressions for this appetite as well - eating so much chocolate that it makes me sick, stealing chocolate to eat, eating chocolate in front of my friend and not sharing and thus hurting our relationship, eating so much chocolate I don't eat any other food, or perhaps eating chocolate when I have a chocolate allergy.

This may sound excessive when thinking about chocolate, but these are the boundaries that I think it's good to ask for any expression of any appetite to make sure that it's within an ethical framework that works for you.

Questions for Healthy Kink

Does it honor your relationship with God? I'm not going to pretend that everyone reading this book has the same relationship with God and scripture that I do, but I assume that you have some view of God and scripture. And I think that everyone can agree that there are some kinks and practices that don't have an ethical and righteous expression, and people's opinions of those are going to be different for different people. Some expressions of some kinks are unethical, dangerous, and even illegal. Any righteous expression of a practice or kink that you have has to honor your relationship with God, your ethics, and your interpretation with scripture. For me, some boundaries feel easy for me to set - ones like all kinky practices take place within my marriage and involve only my husband and I, for instance, but others are more difficult.

One such boundary that I wasn't expecting involved one of my favorite fantasies which I have mentioned before, which involves me doing something wrong and being punished for it. I love reading this scenario, I love writing this, and it sounds like it would be deliciously fun in real life. But in working this out in real life, I found that this doesn't align with how I view God, relationship with my husband, and scripture. As I talked about in a previous chapter, if my husband were to punish me for wrongdoing, this would be putting my husband in a place of authority over me, which does not align with my interpretation of scripture. My interpretation of scripture is that we are to be equal partners, co-heirs both made in the image of God and to submit to one another mutually. Ethically speaking, having one spouse punish the other one would put them in a place not of mutually submissive partnership, but more in the place reserved for a parent or God. I'm not saying that for another couple that had another type of interpretation of scripture and biblical marriage, it might be different, but this is how my husband and I interpret scripture and apply it to our lives.

When my husband and I first started exploring my kink, I tried to make this fantasy work in real life, but I was never able to do it because the Spirit inside me resisted to the point that I knew it to be wrong. My husband and I talked about it, and we realized that there was no way that I could do this kink in a real way that would work with our view of scripture and our theology about marriage. This is a kink and a yearning that has no righteous expression in real life, so it's not something that I can do in reality. We have found ways that I can play-act it and do on occasion, but that is where this kink ends for me. This is similar to a couple that might want to explore a scenario where the husband picks up a strange woman in the bar, and his wife poses as that strange woman.

Does it dishonor my body and person? I have read things that people have written that said that activities should never leave a mark or cause pain, and in some ways, I laugh a bit at that. Does that mean I should never ride my bike because I often bark my shins on the pedals? There was a lot of pain when I set the goal of a two-mile swim across a local lake a few years ago, and nobody discouraged me because I was sore for days after I did my accomplishment. And I'm not athletic - I have a friend who rock-climbs and always seems to have new marks on him. But on the other hand, if you had a friend that was rock-climbing in such a way that he was always so beat up he couldn't work, you would seriously question whether rock-climbing was a good hobby. Pain can be experienced differently when it is accompanied by pleasure, as any mountain biker or surfer can tell you. But it needs to be done in a way that honors your body. What are your limits? What feels good? Are there things that don't?

For me, this has meant that I have found implements that cause pain but no marks, but if there's someone that wants to have a few marks, then I think that's completely fine for that couple. Don't push your body past where it can go, either emotionally or physically. It also needs to honor your personhood - and this is a little trickier. It is not unusual when you find something new that you love to become very excited about it, whether it's a new hobby or a new baby. And just like when you have a new baby you need to talk about things other than the baby; as you explore parts of your kink, you need to make sure that it doesn't take over too much of your life. Make sure you have a sex life apart from your kink, and relationship apart from your kink. Back to the example of the chocolate - it's not healthy if your entire diet is chocolate; you need a variety.

Does it honor your relationship with your spouse? Part of this kink is that it often involves two people, and whatever you do should honor the relationship between you. That means that whatever you do has to be a negotiation between the two of you, and it should honor both people. That doesn't mean that both people need to be fulfilled through the kink, just like there's a lot of vanilla type sexual activity that is about pleasing one partner at a time. But neither should something be repulsive to the person, difficult, or traumatizing. Care should also be taken to make sure that everyone "has their cookies" as well.

My husband is vanilla, but he is a good sport. We will take a night away from our kids and stay in a hotel several times a year, and prior to my revelations about my kink, these nights usually involved a nice dinner, some extra care and time given around our lovemaking, and maybe some new lingerie. After my revelation, things got a little spicier. For special nights away with my husband, I began to plan elaborate costumes, write out scenarios, and try new implements. I would spend the week before our encounter dreaming about our encounter, and the week after in post-encounter bliss. And through it all he has figured it out - learning the technique on how to spank me how I wanted it, visiting a sex shop with me to buy a paddle (that's a crazy story in and of itself; I'll tell you about it in the implementation section), believing me when I tell him that hurting can feel good, and never once questioning my mental health. But, as he's not a kinky person, he needs some extra attention during our encounters to make it enjoyable for him as well.

Righteous Expression

Not all fantasies or kinks have a righteous expression, and that's okay. It doesn't mean that you're a bad person or a wrong person; it just means that fulfilling that fantasy doesn't have a healthy option for you right now. For most people, there will be some option for the expression of their kink that will make them feel that they are living ethically and holistically. You're not a bad person for wanting to eat a lot of chocolate, but if you're allergic to it, then you need to find other options. And even if you're not allergic, moderation is key.

When I was single and before I told my husband about my kink, my main option for my kink was writing stories, and I felt a great deal of shame over this. Now, looking back, I think it was an acceptable expression. It didn't dishonor my relationship with God or with myself, nor did it dishonor my future husband. My stories were of the *Little House on the Prairie* or *Treasure Island* sort of variety, except there were more spankings in them. I found I wrote as little as possible, just enough to get by and satisfy enough of my kink not to go completely crazy. But then, shortly before I came out to my husband, I discovered Harry Potter fanfiction.

I have always loved Harry Potter, and one night when I was browsing the internet, I stumbled onto fanfiction, and I felt like my world changed. I had written fanfiction on my own, even fanfiction related to Harry Potter, but I didn't realize that other people did it. I read other stories that people wrote, and they were remarkably similar to mine, and I felt such a kinship, such a sense of belonging, and a feeling of home. I read everything I could find in this genre, and then tentatively starting posting. Posting fanfiction was an incredible step forward in owning my orientation - not only was I stepping forward, getting feedback on my stories, developing a thick skin when trolls made horrible comments about me, interacting with readers, and being myself. I think this freedom I found writing fanfiction helped me be honest with myself and then with my husband. When I could tell a troll that I wasn't sick in the head for writing a story containing spanking in it, I was telling myself that as well.

Children

As a therapist, I tell parents that all of the experts find that spanking is not a helpful form of discipline; it causes shame and harm to the child and increases aggression. As someone with a spanking kink, I know that it can also be something else for kids like me; it can be harm against my sexuality.

One writer that I've read calls it sexual abuse to spank a kinky child and uses that as an argument not to spank any child,[28] and I'm not sure I would go that far. But I will tell you that I avoided real disciplinary spankings at all costs as a child, and found the few I received to be traumatizing. The times I have witnessed a child getting a swat or two in real life have not at all triggered my kink, and I have found it off-putting. And just so I'm clear on this, I have chosen not to spank my children.

Chapter 9:

Christian Domestic Discipline - Living in Denial

If you haven't heard of Christian Domestic Discipline (CDD) yet, you are in for a real mind-bender. I first heard of it several years ago when several articles were floating around mainstream media,[29] and I was at once attracted and repulsed. I felt like this was such a very good fantasy but a very bad reality.

The idea of CDD is that the man of the house is what's called the Head of House (HOH), and he's in complete charge, and his job is to make sure his subordinates in the house (which includes his wife and children) obey him. He uses punishments to keep everyone in line, both with his children and his wife. This usually includes spanking as one of the primary forms of discipline, both in response to what the HOH decides is misbehavior and as what is called "maintenance spankings." This is seen as a biblical lifestyle, as a living example of Godly submission in marriage.

Horseshit.

If you knew me in real life and realized how rarely I swore (I think I just used up my one free swear a year on that), you would realize how strongly worded that epitaph was. Couples that live this lifestyle are living it for two reasons: either the husband is an abuser or the couple is kinky. And from most of the sites I read, I think it's mostly due to the latter. CDD is not a biblical lifestyle; it is a couple living a kink and not wanting to admit it, and using the veil of Christianity to hide their proclivities behind. I've read what feels like millions of these sites with people proclaiming this lifestyle and women asking questions about living this lifestyle, and I've myself longed to live this lifestyle, and I think that this is just one way for people to live in denial that can't face their sexual identity. Here is the evidence from a variety of websites supporting this lifestyle:

Maintenance Spankings: These are spankings that are used to "remind the wife of consequences of bad behavior" and to reinforce what might happen if she were to misbehave. These spankings are supposed to be lighter than punishment spankings, but still enough to sting. This is essentially acknowledging that the couple is into spanking; you wouldn't do maintenance spankings if spanking was a punishment. Use this logic for something that is a punishment and see how it goes. "Timmy, you haven't been bad today, but I feel like I have to remind you that I'm in charge, and to behave yourself, so you're grounded from your bike this afternoon." Or for an adult, "Sir, I'm pulling you over today and giving you a ticket not because you were speeding but to remind you not to speed should you be tempted to do it."

Spanking Porn - These sites often have tons of spanking porn on them, either with stories or pictures. It's often titled "romantic fiction" or something and propped up as something supporting the lifestyle, but I don't buy it. I'm not saying that I don't

78

appreciate a good spanking story, but if this were punishment, wouldn't you dislike it? In more recent years, there has been less of this on Christian Domestic Discipline sites, probably in response to critics saying just this. But on non-Christian sites, there is still much of this going on. If spanking were an unwanted punishment, then it wouldn't be considered romantic and sexy. When was the last time you put a speeding ticket in the drawer beside your bed?

Kinky Identity - Many women who are involved in this lifestyle talk about how they've always longed for this lifestyle and have thought about spanking their whole life - and it is often the woman who brings this idea into the relationship. When women are directly asked questions regarding if spanking is a kink for them or if there's something enjoyable, they often say something along the lines of, "Nobody enjoys a spanking, but afterward I feel closer to my husband because it feels so good to be protected and guided," or something to that effect. The phrase "Nobody enjoys a spanking" happens on these sites all the time, almost like an agreed talisman against anybody knowing deeper secrets about them, even though they have to know that MANY PEOPLE DO! If people didn't, why do they have spanking porn on their site? Have they looked around at general society? Do they not know that it is one of the most common fantasies that people have? Also, the Q & A sections on these sites have three main questions from women: asking how to ask their husbands to live this kind of lifestyle, what to do if they are single and long to live this lifestyle, and how to handle it if there's no reason to be spanked and the wife wants a spanking (also called "bratting").

Consent and autonomy - I work with victims of domestic violence, and there are specific markers that you look for in relationships that contain DV. There have been many times I'm the first person to tell a girl or woman that she might consider whether or not her partner might be abusing her. I'm not going to make a blanket statement and say that every relationship that says it uses

CDD doesn't have elements of DV, because I'm sure some do, especially ones that aren't being advertised via blogs and websites. But DV usually looks very different than what I see portrayed by what women write on the websites. I want to be very careful here because I'm sure some women have been victimized by abusers under the guise of CDD. But the blogs I have read and the people that advocate for CDD publicly are not those people - these bloggers are into it. There is consent, and there is autonomy. The wife often is the one who instigated the whole thing. The wife could end it if she chose to, and she is choosing not to end it because it fulfills her kink. There is no DV cycle of abuse, there is none of the gaslighting and emotional abuse that I look for in a typical case of DV; instead, it looks pretty straightforward and pretty kinky.

I didn't write this chapter to say that people can't live a CDD lifestyle if they didn't want to; I just think that if people want to live this lifestyle, they should be honest about why they are doing so. This isn't in adherence to their interpretation of the bible; it is in adherence to their kink. I think it's completely fine to live in adherence to your kink, and it's even preferable than trying to suppress it, but I think people should do so in an honest way. And if those bloggers that are being so open about their "biblical" lifestyle instead were more honest about their orientation and kink, it would make the world a little safer for others that shared it.

I also want to say that whenever people use religion in a relationship where there can be a power differential, the situation can be ripe for abuse. Jim Alsdurf, a forensic psychologist who treats sexual psychopaths and author of a book about abuse in Christian homes, goes a lot further. He says, "A relationship that infantilizes a woman is one that clearly draws a more pathological group of people . . . If people want to spank each other, go ahead. The problem of course, is if it's done in a controlling and mildly abusive way. If they're not done healthily, they can become about abuse and control."[30]

I also feel obliged to say at the end of this chapter that if you are being abused by an intimate partner, it is not your fault; please get help. You can contact a local women's shelter anonymously, and they are happy to help you make a plan to get safe. You don't deserve to be abused. In the US, the national crisis line for domestic violence is 1-800-799-7233.

Chapter 10:

Spanking While Being Single

In writing this chapter, I would like to acknowledge that it has been a long time since I was single; I was married in my late twenties. At the time, I felt that I was quite old, as I was the oldest first-time bride in the history of my family, but now I look back and feel like I was just a baby when I walked down that aisle in my white dress on my father's arm. I also did live for many years after that in secrecy - which is a form of being single, in my kink, at least. I want to write to single people - either single without a partner entirely or single without a partner that can participate in this kink with them. Because many, many kinksters long for partners and have that longing unfulfilled.

First, I want to say that Paul affirms being single as a very godly and good state to be in, and sees it as a gift. He affirms that it gives you more undivided time for God's work in the world and that you can be more concerned with pleasing God than pleasing your spouses and children. However, it is not a command to stay single, and he acknowledges that many people don't have the gift of singleness.[31]

Whether or not you feel that your singleness is a gift or not, whether it's a gift that will be lifelong or of a shorter duration, if you have a spanking kink, then this chapter is for you. All of us have times of singleness in our lives, but if you're kinky, then you are always kinky and that doesn't go away just because you got divorced, widowed, or haven't found the right partner yet.

So how do you deal with your kink when you have nobody to share it with? Here are the options as I see them, and the pros and cons of each:

Option 1: Denial and Suppression

I lived this option for so many years. If you are currently living this option, my heart goes out to you. This is such a hard place to be, and sometimes it can feel so holy as if you are denying yourself and picking up the cross. The problem is, to live a more holy lifestyle, your brain and body rarely cooperate. And, if you're reading this book, I'm guessing yours didn't either.

At one point, I burned my stories, destroying the thirty-something notebooks I'd been filling with spanking stories since my teens. I thought it would be an act of worship, a showing of my dedication to God. I thought that through my sacrifice, I would be healed; I thought that through the fire, I would be cleansed. And I did learn something through those flames - and I learned something very valuable about God. I learned that we do not control our redemption and that we do not get to just destroy our shame and not deal with it. God was very gentle and kind to me during this time, but there was no magic formula that kink was burned from my life just as surely as those spiral-bound notebooks on that May evening deep in the woods. And now, with no stories to read and a strict new policy I had imposed on myself of no writing, the stories began to rattle around in my head with no place to go. I would dream of my stories, and my traitorous thoughts would dwell on them whenever I had moments of boredom in class or at work. I found myself typing the beginnings of the stories forming in my mind, and then castigating myself and deleting them in shame.

The pros to this way of dealing with your kink are very few; in fact, the only pro I can think of is that you might feel more godly. I didn't feel godly; I felt like a huge sinner and fraud. I had equated my stories and my kink with sin, and I felt powerless to conquer it. The cons to this option I believe are huge. This level of denial of your identity, I think, has a very harsh effect on your sense of personhood and your relationship with Jesus. If Jesus came to deliver us from sin and we equate some innate part of ourselves with sin, then how can we ever be free? I felt as powerless to change this part of myself as I felt the ability to change my eye color. Sure, I could wear contacts, so I looked different from the world, but my real eye color didn't change at all.

Option 2: A Rich Fantasy Life

I grew into Option 2 out of desperation. This is the option I utilized most of my childhood, and I reverted to it after several years in Option 1 just because I couldn't handle it anymore. I wrote stories for my own writing and reading pleasure and read normal fiction that contained spankings. My stories contained no sex because I hadn't yet understood that part of my sexuality, and most of the stories I found online that contained spankings weren't really to my taste. So I stayed in my fantasy world and enjoyed it. When I found fanfiction, my world changed immensely, and I began sharing my stories with others and enjoying stories others wrote. I write much more about this in the chapter about coming out if you're interested.

The pros to this are that I felt like I could satisfy my kink and not cross any boundaries that I set for myself around issues like pornography. I found writing my stories to be pretty satisfying to my kink, especially once I got into fanfiction and could read and write with other people similar to myself. The cons are very few, except that it doesn't satisfy that longing for a partner. Also, you have to be careful if you're worried about the fear of discovery if you share a computer.

Option 3: Self-Spanking

This is not an option I've done a lot of, but I thought it would be a good one to mention in case it would be helpful to someone. To be honest, I mostly did it just because I was curious and because I was trying to write a description of a spanking and felt that I wasn't describing things properly because I hadn't experienced it. It's pretty much exactly what it sounds like - you spank yourself. It works best with something like a hairbrush or wooden spoon.

I think there are pros if you are into it, and some people are when I researched it. It can feel like a normal spanking, which is a pro. The con is that it is awkward, and if you are the one spanking yourself, there's not a real feeling of surrender that can feel so good during a typical spanking. There can also be a "this is weird" feeling that can be a con to it as well, though if you were giving yourself a deep tissue massage on your thigh nobody would think twice, so don't let that stop you.

Option 4: Finding Someone to Spank You

This option has the highest pro in that it is a real spanking, but it also has the highest cons. This is the riskiest of the options, as it often involves a rather intimate thing with a relative stranger. It is also something that is/can be relatively sexually charged, and it can be for your partner, even if it's not for you. You also have to ask yourself if you think it would satisfy you if it's not someone you have a more intimate relationship with - for someone with this kink, spanking usually is a very intimate thing. For me, being spanked by someone other than my husband would feel like a violation.

If you do decide to go ahead with it, make sure it's a safe situation and make sure it doesn't violate your ethics in any way. Set firm, clear boundaries that you expect to be followed that are negotiated ahead of time.

Chapter 11:

Coming Out

Your Intimate Partner

Dear Vivian,

This is your future self from five years from now. For you to know that this is really me, let's just say I know about that "spanking sin" you're always so worried about but have never told anyone about except your college mentor a bit, and we both know you chickened out on the most shameful parts of that confession.

So here's the thing, I know that you've been agonizing on whether or not to tell hubby about all your stuff. You envision this going one of two ways: He could either go with it and be supportive, or he could think you are sick and twisted and even those love pats he sometimes gives you might go away. But worse, his rejection of that secret, inner part of you would hurt so bad that you don't think you could survive it.

So much to lose, so much to gain. You wish you could say it and go back in time if it goes badly, but unfortunately, magic doesn't exist. You've spent years hinting and hoping that you wouldn't have to be brave and tell him, but at some point, you will either have to tell him or resign yourself to a life lived with this secret hidden from the man you love and trust the most.

Think about how he has been when he's found out other things about you - has he condemned you? Has he used information against you and ridiculed you? Has he kept your confidence?

I am not going to tell you how it turned out because you deserve to make this decision without any future knowledge. But remember the quote from one of your favorite movies - "A life lived in fear is a life half lived."[32]

Good Luck.

Future Vivian

Telling your partner or other people in your life can be very frightening. I know that it took me fourteen years of loving, trusting marriage to get to the point that I could do it. My husband had never given me a reason to think that he would shame me and make me feel bad for how I was, but I was already doing enough shaming of myself that it was hard to believe that he wouldn't do it as well. It wasn't until I found the comradery of the Harry Potter fanfiction and realized that there were more people like me that I began to think that this part of me might be okay. With my daughters, I spent so much time talking to them about accepting the bodies that God had given them - hair, butts, skin, and everything. I told them that true peace comes when we realize that the body that God has given us is what He has given us and that we are beautiful how we are. Why couldn't I give the same grace to my psyche? I had tried to give up writing, and it hadn't worked, and I recognized that maybe that's not what God wanted for me. Maybe what He wanted was for me to find peace another way - not by "curing" me of my kink, but instead with me making peace with it. And I couldn't be friends with my kink without introducing my husband to it.

In the end, I did tell my husband; and as you already know, he handled it well. He is what the BDSM world calls vanilla - in that he doesn't have any kink himself. But he understands that it is something that I want and crave, and he is willing to learn and to participate in it to make me happy. It's not to say the journey has been completely smooth - it took him a while to understand that I did want it to hurt a bit, and that seemed hard for him to grasp at first. But once he chose to believe me and saw my reaction, well, he became convinced.

The best advice for telling your partner is to find a good time when you are both relaxed and tell them in a way that doesn't communicate that they have to participate if they want to stay with you, but rather that this is something you'd like to explore if they're up for it. The more at peace you are about going into it, the better. If you are a bundle of nerves and shame, it will be a lot harder on the both of you. You need to respect your partner's boundaries as well, if they really can't participate in your fantasies, then there has to be a mutually respectful way to move forward with that. But even if that's the case, talking about those fantasies will increase intimacy and understanding between you.

You can also start with micro-disclosures - maybe suggesting trying a very mild and socially acceptable version of something you'd be into and seeing if your partner would like to try it. Eventually, you have to be brave and be honest, but this can sometimes be a good on-ramp.

Telling Others

Studies show that most kinky people do tell their intimate partners, but are at least partially closeted in other parts of their lives. Even though after the publication of *50 Shades of Grey* there has been more discussion in popular culture about BDSM than there ever was before, this is still a pretty taboo topic. Kinky people say that they've faced discrimination in the workplace, medical care, psychological care, in child custody cases, and with their families.

"Coming out" is often not a positive experience for many people with this kink, and people are aware of the stigmas.[33] I have chosen not to tell many people in my life, but part of that is the cost I could pay if it became widely known. Given my profession, I fear that there could be a cost for me professionally, and being part of a conservative Christian community makes me weigh the cost there as well.

Many kinky people are very careful whom they tell, but here is a list of people that you should at least consider:

Your Spouse - Well, for obvious reasons, as they are probably who you would like to play and act out your fantasies with.

Your Therapist - But only if the person seems open to not stigmatizing this sexual expression. See the chapter called "Spanking and Psychology" for more details.

Your Doctor - This is not necessary, but helpful if you are doing anything that might leave a mark that might make your doctor think you're in an abusive relationship. A heads-up might save you some rather pointed questions and embarrassment, or even a call to the police.

Your Best Friend - Again, this isn't necessary, but it might be good to have someone to talk to and to affirm you when you're feeling like a freak. This is especially true for the single kinkster.

Writing Fanfiction

If you want to find my fanfiction, you can - my author's name is RainCityWriter, and I publish on Fanfiction.net. I will say that if you're looking for racy, romantic stories, you're out of luck; my fanfiction is all very innocent and most of the "Snape spanks Harry" variety of Harry Potter fanfiction. But I wanted to write about writing fanfiction in this chapter because writing fanfiction for me was a lot about coming out, even though I did it under a false name, and only my husband knows that I write it.

It is an incredible act of bravery for anybody to put their work out online for people to read it, and a site like Fanfiction.net can be particularly brutal. For those unfamiliar with how it works, the author posts their story, usually one chapter at a time, and people online from around the world read it and offer feedback. Some feedback is completely innocuous, often, "Update soon!" Some are incredibly detailed with an intimate discussion of your characters, their motivations, and speculations on where you are going next in your story. Some commentators on fanfiction have become online friends and writing partners, especially those that are fellow writers themselves. And then there are what the internet charmingly calls trolls.

For my sanity, I like to picture trolls as twenty-three-year-old, pale, pimply-faced antisocial cretins who live in their parents' basements and who don't have anything better to do than to torture authors of fanfiction. I'm not sure if there are other subtypes of fanfiction that get the types of trolling that discipline fiction gets, but I was a little unprepared for the onslaught of truly horrendous comments. And I'm not talking about comments critical of my grammar or typos, or even my overall characterization or story arc - those are fair criticisms, and while they aren't fun to get, they are useful and respectful. I'm talking about repeated comments calling me sick, depraved, a child abuser, and worse. My stories are clearly marked as containing spanking, a common and legal practice in schools at the period when Harry Potter takes place, yet still many anonymous (and a few non-anonymous ones) attacked me for it. And it's not just me; authors don't warn readers if they are going to torture or kill a character, but if there's going to be a spanking, they often feel that they had better warn you in at least three places before it happens.

The first several troll comments I got made me feel terrible - was I traumatizing people by what I was writing? Was I really the crazy pervert people were accusing me of being? Should I stop posting the stories that spilled out of my head without control sometimes? Some matter of months after I told my husband the truth, something changed within me. It was gradual, and not in response to anyone comment in particular. But there was one comment that stuck in my head, and it was something along the lines of, "Do your parents know what you write? You are sick!" And this struck me as so incongruous because I was likely at least ten years older than the person who wrote the comment. And let me be clear, my fanfiction stories are very clean and innocent - nothing happens in them that doesn't happen in the stories I grew up reading like *Little House on the Prairie*, except that the spankings are more frequent.

And then I did something, which was something that claimed my dignity back from those pimply-faced basement dwellers. I wrote an ironic story I called "Harry Potter and the Controversial Strawberries." It was a short story about a conversation between Harry and his friends and Snape, talking about how silly it was that people freak out about food allergies as people do to strawberries (strawberries being the obvious stand-in for spankings). But then the main reason that I wrote the story was to mock the trolls, and that was where I had fun. Here's a selection of the "troll" comments:

Comment: *You're a pervert! Did someone force you to eat strawberries as a child?*

Comment: *I've read every word you've ever written, including stories that are 37 chapters long, and I'm just so offended that you would include strawberries. There must be something wrong with you that you want to write about strawberries all the time. Apparently, there's nothing else to read, and I must read your stories, so make them how I want them and stop offending me.*

Comment: *I haven't actually read your work, but the fact that there is the word "strawberries" in your description means that I would like to discuss how my political agenda would ban all strawberries from first-world nations because who cares about the strawberries in poorer countries.*

Comment: *I would never trust you to raise a child! How could you let them contemplate eating strawberries so brazenly! Don't you know that some children are abused by strawberries! Some are allergic! People could be triggered by reading this!*

Comment: *Do your parents know that you are obsessed with strawberries? Or was it because they gave you strawberries as a child that you feel like you need to write about them?*

Comment: *Even though strawberries were perfectly common and legal the year that your source material took place and even hinted at in the source material, how dare you write about strawberries!*

Comment: *You just write about strawberries to get sick freaks to read your stories, you review monger.*

Fanfiction seems like a very strange way of coming out and owning my own identity, but I slowly but surely did. As time went on, I just posted one warning at the beginning of my story, announced that I took my troll immunity potion, and honestly began to care less and less when the trolls came to call. I set an easy protocol and guideline on which reviews got deleted - if they personally attacked readers or me with my kink, they were gone. If they were critical of my work, as long as they didn't do any personal attacks, then that was fine. And for someone for whom words mean an incredible amount, that was amazing growth indeed.

Chapter 12

Sexual Response

This chapter is going to talk scientifically accurately as well as pretty bluntly about sex. There's nothing in this chapter that isn't in scientific journals and anatomy books, but if you're a bit squeamish, I'll understand if you give this chapter a pass and go on to the next one.

Not every kinky person has a sexual response to a spanking; sometimes spanking inhibits a different part of their psyche. For my entire growing up, I didn't realize how linked it was to my sexuality, and the only reason I thought that there might be as an adult was just that so much of modern culture seemed to link the two things. It wasn't until I went in real life with my kink that I had any idea of the depth of my sexual response to it.

The first time my husband spanked me, I was shocked at the response my body had sexually. I knew I had always craved spanking, but I didn't realize it as a sexual thing in my body. But when he gave me those first few awkward swats with his hand, and in the heady endorphins of telling someone for the first time about my secret shame and having him accept it so thoroughly, my body was rocked with an intense and radically different sort of orgasm when we had sex shortly afterward. This orgasm was something that felt so different than what I'd experienced from the typical ones I'd been having for years. Why was this experience so different for me? I had always orgasmed fairly easily with a few techniques picked up from good Christian books about love and marriage that our pastor recommended to us before marriage. Even on my wedding night, we were able to get there eventually, after the first frantic and excited coupling that was thrilling until it hurt. Orgasms were sometimes elusive - such as when I was pregnant and felt ready to puke with the rocking motion from sex. But for the most part, we enjoyed a regular sex life and regular, consistent orgasms. So what happened?

The Link of Kink and Sex

Women's sexual lives are complex and vary greatly. There's a reason that there's no Viagra equivalent for women - and it boils down to two very important things about women's sexual responses. One, women's bodies vary more than men's do in sexual response mechanisms and how they respond sexually. What works for one woman doesn't work for another. The second is that for women, sex is very contextual - how women feel about sex is the most important factor for them. So for women, it's less a matter of hormones and nervous system responses than it is about their emotional reality. "Which means that stress, mood, trust, and body image are not peripheral factors in a woman's sexual wellbeing; they are central to it."[34] I would also say that for a lot of women, exploration of their kink has a lot of the same factors that sex does for them - stress, mood, trust, and body image all play a role in the experience for them.

Kinky men, though their response is less complex than women's, clearly also have a response that is more than hormones and tactile response. The part of kink that is about the mind and emotions is enormous and cannot be overstated.

Types of Orgasms

For me, an orgasm from a spanking felt different - deeper, intense in a different way, and a different area and my body created a crazy amount of lubrication. After reading research and carefully tuning in to my body during sex with spankings and sex without spankings, often right after each other in the same encounter, I figured out a name that worked for me for each. Spanking triggered what I called "G-spot orgasms," and sex without spanking led to orgasms that were centered around my clitoris, which were intense and started there but spread down my thighs, and would often peak again at least two or three times as we finished up sex. G-spot orgasms were reliable and incredibly quick to induce - I could go from zero to orgasm in just a few minutes. Clitoral orgasms were on their schedule - I would get there eventually, but I had to wait and be patient. Orgasms are like snowflakes; no two are alike for any woman, and women's experiences vary greatly. However, for me, having some categories to think about my sexual response was helpful.

I chose my words carefully with what I called my two different types of orgasms because there is a long and misogynistic history of differentiating between types of orgasms for women. Freud said in 1905 that there were two types of orgasms in women, and he said with no supporting evidence that what he called vaginal orgasms (those resulting from penile penetration only) were superior and the result of maturity, while clitoral orgasms were a result of immaturity and maybe even mental illness.[35] His speculation led to decades of sexual oppression for women, and it wasn't until the 1950s and 60s that researchers began to recognize the clitoris as the main organ of female sexual response. Now, most researchers discount Freud altogether and realize that sexual response is a lot more complex than just two options. And some women do experience two different types of orgasms as I do, and some experience different intensities and levels of orgasms based on the foreplay given. There is still a lot of controversy over many of these issues - whether the G spot exists, whether women ejaculate, what is the role exactly of the clitoris in orgasm, the purpose of the female orgasm, and how it works.[36] Adding to this controversy is the difficulty that women vary so much from person to person on how they are built and how they respond sexually, that there is no one right answer that's right for everyone.

BDSM as a Non-Sexual Practice

People who engage in all different practices of BDSM sometimes engage in sex around these practices, and sometimes don't. Many clubs and spaces where people go to practice and meet partners with which to play have strict no-sex rules, and the play focuses entirely on BDSM activities. A lot of fantasies about BDSM are also not sexual, and there is a lot about BDSM that doesn't feel sexual to practitioners.

I believe that kinksters can live for many years, perhaps even their whole lives without their kink being part of their sexual practices. The problem with this, however, is that it so often is part of sexual practice that it can be hard to do it as a partner activity if it's not sexual.

Anal Sex

I wanted to put a section in here on anal sex just because that is another sexual practice that has been much maligned by the Christian church, probably because of its association with homosexuality. While not technically BDSM, it can be involved in several BDSM practices. Vanilla people and homosexual people have anal sex as well, so it's not exclusively BDSM, but it's common in the BDSM world. So I thought it would be good to talk a little bit more about it.

First off: theology. Even according to the great "Can we _____?" theologians Mark and Grace Driscoll, the bible doesn't have anything to say against anal sex, though the Driscolls still hint that it's not a great idea.[37] There's nothing in the bible against a married man and woman having anal sex, the only prohibitions are about homosexual sex, and even then mostly it's about temple prostitution and rape. As discussed in a previous chapter, the Bible is remarkably silent on matters relevant to marital sex - as long as it is consensual, promotes intimacy, and pursues fulfillment, then it is biblical. As long as those conditions are met, then it is fine to pursue. But if anything about anal sex goes against the ethics of either party or it feels as if it interferes with marital intimacy, then it is not a good idea.

Practicalities: I once had a client come into session after being in a new relationship and being pressured to try anal sex for the first time. Her boyfriend pressured her in the middle of sex, she agreed to try it, and it hurt and caused bleeding. I have heard similar stories before, and I'm always shocked by how people try anal sex like this with no preparation. Anal sex cannot be tried like this; trying it carelessly can lead to scary-sounding things like anal fissures, bleeding, infection, and pain. However done well, it can be a pleasant and very unique experience. The best advice for anal sex is to treat it completely differently from vaginal sex: go very slowly and use fingers or toys before introducing something larger like a penis. Lube is not optional; it is essential. The anus doesn't produce its own lubrication like the vagina does, so you must introduce lubrication. There has to be good communication between the partners to do this, as penetration and thrusting will be very different than it is for vaginal sex. Also, be very careful of hygiene - if you are doing anal sex, then don't switch to vaginal sex without thorough sanitizing because you don't want to transfer bacteria between the two. One great place to explore anal sex is in the shower together.

Oral Sex

Oral sex has a long and sordid history of Christians not being okay with it, though in recent years, most large Christian organizations have mostly endorsed oral sex as long as both parties consent and the partners are married. The argument against it is mostly that it is a sexual practice that doesn't result directly in impregnation, so it must be wrong. This is one of the least controversial sexual practices, though if you do Google "Kinky Christian sex," you will likely come up with references to oral sex, because for many people that is as kinky as it gets.

Toys

In the age of Amazon, people that would normally be too shy to go into a sex shop to buy toys can shop for them in the comfort of their own home. So here are a couple of different categories of toys to think about that you might enjoy.

Spanking Implements - The obvious toy for this book, but in all seriousness, there are quite a few different types of spanking implements to try. Check out the following chapter for some different ones to try.

Butt plugs - These are fairly self-explanatory, but they are plugs that go in your anus. They come in many different sizes, materials, and some even vibrate. Good for men and women! When used during sex, they provide a very different type of feeling, and they can also help stretch you out and get you ready for anal sex.

Make sure you use the type that has a ring or something at the end so they don't go all the way in! As with anything anal, use lube!

Vibrators - Some people find these very helpful when the woman is having trouble reaching orgasm or when her partner is away. If you have neither of these problems, I would give caution in using them, however, because you don't want to become dependent on them for orgasms. Sometimes women even report that they can reduce sensitivity. But if you need some help getting there, these can be invaluable.

Costumes - These can be fun when you are setting the mood for an encounter. Sometimes dreaming about the encounter can be a lot of the fun of having the encounter, and picking your costume is part of that.

Bondage equipment - Handcuffs, scarves, ropes, etc. can all be part of your arsenal if you're into bondage.

Lubricant - You don't think of lubricant as a toy, but it can be an essential part of your enjoyment. Make sure it's going to be one that doesn't bother your skin but is effective.

A word to those with children - please make sure that if you have toys or costumes or anything like that, you are either good at hiding things or you have a locked box in which you keep things. I have known too many people that are horrified when their child finds something that they don't want to explain. I also think the best sex toy we ever got was a lock for our bedroom door - there is comfort and security in knowing that a child can't accidentally walk in on us! I had a real problem keeping my kids from walking in on me dressing, so I explained to our kids that the lock is for when I'm changing my clothes. So it's really easy if a kid knocks while we're, um, not wanting to be disturbed that I'll just say I'm changing and will be with them in a minute.

Chapter 13

Nuts and Bolts of a Spanking

This is probably the chapter that's the most fun to write, as it's all fun and no heavy thinking. Again, I would like to preface this chapter that it's all based on my own experiences, and your mileage may vary a lot. This is the part that's supposed to be fun and playful - experiment and play! This chapter is going to be pretty honest and straightforward about how the basics of this works, so if you don't want to read about the graphic details you can give this chapter a pass.

Safety

Safeword - You should always have a safeword that is established between you, either something that you say that ends the play or a word. Some couples like to pretend to protest the spanking, so having words other than typical protest words can be helpful. A really common word to use is "red" like a stoplight, and then you have the benefit of using "yellow" to mean caution that you are getting close to needing to use red. It's also considered bad manners for the top to push the bottom to use the safeword regularly; it should be a rare occurrence. Open communication can also be just as effective, as in saying, "Hey baby, let's do a few more swats, but maybe not quite so hard."

Research and Education - Several practices in the BDSM world require education and research to do properly, and if those are one of your kinks, please do the research! Even simple things like spanking require some research to do properly - where on the buttocks do you strike to not hurt the recipient of the spanking? How does the spanker hold their hand to minimize pain for them? Some implements require more skill than others - for instance, a belt requires more skill than a paddle. Bondage requires some skill to restrain someone without restricting their blood supply. Whatever kink you want to try or a new activity you want to experiment with, make sure that you research it thoroughly with both partners, establish safety guidelines, and do it carefully.

Communication - This is key to any kink practice. Both people practicing a kink need to be listening, communicating, and making their needs and wants known to the other. I once heard sex columnist Dan Savage say that a gift he wanted to give heterosexuals from the homosexual community was the gift of negotiating sex. He said that before any sex in the homosexual community, there is a negotiation - usually in the form of the question, "What are you into?" In the heterosexual community, sex is usually more straightforward, and therefore there tends to be less communication. In the kink community, there is also negotiation and communication that is necessary before any kink happens, and this is important and good for the relationship. "What are you feeling like tonight?" is a great question to ask your partner when frisky vibes are happening between the two of you. For me, this question from my husband might elicit an answer of, "Actually, tonight I just want sweet, gentle sex," or it might be, "Hmm, feeling pretty naughty," or, "I would love a spanking, but maybe a gentle one, just with your hand?"

Spanking Positions

This might seem not as obvious to someone who hasn't experimented much with spanking, but there are several different positions and pros and cons for each one. Before I started being spanked, most of my fantasies centered around being spanked on someone's lap. I have to admit that it still is a very nice position for me, but there are pros and cons to each one. There are a lot of different positions, but they mostly boil down to three practical ones (and a few less practical ones that I will mention):

Over the lap: This is the classic position that most people think of with spanking, where the spanker is sitting down on something, and the person being spanked puts their tummy down across their thighs. A harsh version of this position is on an armless chair where the person being spanked is left dangling a bit with their head and legs bent far down and their bottom in the air. A less harsh version is with the spanker on a bed or couch, and the spankee's legs are down, but their head is on a pillow or something on the couch. This position is nice in that it feels close to the person spanking you. I like this position for long, slow, teasing spanking sessions with lots of hand spankings alternating with a little bit of paddle to heat things up.

Variations: laying over one thigh and having the spanker's other leg "trap" the bottom's legs to prevent kicking, having the bottom straddle one of the top's knees and then laying on the thigh, putting their head on a pillow close to the spanker's hip (the pressure on this one feels good), or having the spanker sit on the bed with their back to the headboard and having the spankee draped across their lap. Cons: This position is very hard to use for implements like the strap, and you have to change position if you want to follow up with sex.

Bent over an object: This works best being bent over a chair, sofa arm, or, most commonly, the edge of the bed. This works for any implement, and also you don't have to change positions to transition into having sex if you want to do so. This also works well for any implement you want to use.

Cons: It feels less intimate than over the lap since you aren't touching during the spanking.

Lying down on the bed or on all fours: These positions are similar and are all variations of the spankee lying down on the bed, either flat, on all fours, or with their head down and their bottom in the air. There's a reason that most classic spanking positions usually involve bending over in some way, and it's because lying down flat (or standing up) doesn't work as well because your muscles will tense differently if you're not bent. So, if you want to be lying down, I suggest some pillows under your hips, so you're not completely flat. This keeps your buttocks from clenching too much, which can make the spanking less enjoyable for both you and your partner.

Positions that are unrealistic or I don't like: Bending over and grabbing your ankles (which is very uncomfortable and easy to be off-balance, which makes you focus more on position than on the spanking); diaper position, which involves the spankee lying on their back with their legs up and the spanker holding their legs to spank them (which I find not very fun); or standing up (doesn't position the buttocks well).

Spanking Target

This may sound a little elementary, but it's good to think about the target of the spanking. It's best to focus most of the spanking on the round part of the cheeks, staying away from the genitals or the upper part of the cheeks where there's less meat. The bottom parts of the cheeks, called the "sit spots," are very tender and should be smacked with care. The upper thighs have less padding and should be smacked with care, as well. The target can be bare or clothed; it's up to the preference of the persons involved. As mentioned in positioning, it's better if the person is bent over, so their muscles are loose and don't clench, and even better if their legs are slightly spread.

Typical Spanking Protocol and Sexual Response

This very much has to do with what a couple finds erotic or part of their fantasy, but this should be something talked about ahead of time. I find it works better to start slow and softer, and "warm-up" the skin. Most couples warm up with hand spanking and then move on to implements after that. Sometimes there is scolding during the spanking, sometimes there is hot sex talk, and sometimes there is laughing and playing. This is completely up to the couple and the preferences that they have. For some people, they like to have a little separation between spanking and sex and don't have them right next to each other. For others, sex is an integral part of spanking, and they wouldn't do one without the other. Sometimes people like a spanking hard and fast with little sexual touching involved, and sometimes a spanking can be a long, drawn-out experience interspersed with sexual touching and massage. How this works between partners is a matter of communication and diplomacy. Most couples like some form of aftercare after the spanking - which could be cuddling, sex, or some form of reassurance. This is usually important for both participants.

Spanking Implements

I'm going to stick to implements that I've used in this section, and acknowledge that there are many more out there that I haven't used. For instance, I have chosen not to use the cane because I didn't want to have marks on me that I would have to explain (I love to swim), and I'm not sure that I want something that hurts that much. The odd bruise isn't hard to explain; I figured stripes would be. This is an area of fun experimentation for you and your partner, so research and find the ones you want to try and what works best for you. I find that most implements are a mixture of what is thought of as "thud" (like a heavy paddle) and a "sting" (like a switch). The best implements are a mixture of both, with some people preferring one to the other. Here are the pros and cons that I've found of each, from mild and then up the intensity ladder:

Hand: This "implement" is easy because it's always there, it's intimate, and it feels good. It's usually what beginners start with for a good reason: it's readily available! There is some technique to be learned here, however, as there are different sensations available. You can try cupping the hand a bit for a different feeling, or relaxing the hand and making it feel a bit more whippy. The hand is good for warm-ups, gentle swats, and beginners.

The cons: It can be hard to up the intensity, and it often hurts the spanker as much as it hurts the spanked.

Ruler: This can be an actual ruler or a paint stirrer from the hardware store. This is free and easy to find, as well as an easy thing to have in your house with no question asked. It is an implement that is stingy rather than thuddy, and it can impart a nice and warm sting on bare skin.

Light Wooden Spoon: This is a step up from a ruler, and it can sting a bit with a very little thud. I'm talking about the one made from bamboo, not the heavy hardwood ones. It is also discreet; almost everybody has one in their kitchen.

Light leather strap: We bought this on Amazon, and it is very stingy as well with a very little thud. It hurts a lot less than we thought it would, but it is still fun to play with. Try to stick to real leather, however, and not plastic, as that can sting in an unpleasant way.

Heavy silicone Spatula: This is where you're getting into the thuddier implements, and this can sting quite a bit when wielded correctly.

Hairbrush: I always used a wooden paddle hairbrush growing up just because I loved thinking about it being a paddle, even though I never had anyone use one on me until my husband did. Hairbrushes can be light and stingy, but mine is heavier and quite thuddy. I like it a lot, but you do have to make sure you get all the hair off of it before your spanking because if you miss a hair, it can tickle. But a hairbrush has the advantage of being non-suspicious to have with you in your luggage or on your dresser, with nobody the wiser.

Leather paddle: This is by far my favorite spanking implement, with just the right mix of thuddy and sting. We bought it on our first weekend away after my big revelation to my husband, and it was before it dawned on us that we could order things off of Amazon. Part of our date was going to a sex shop to buy a paddle to use. To say that this was out of our comfort zone is a massive understatement - we had never done anything like this before, but we were determined to be brave. We went to the section with paddles and floggers, things I had only read about before, and I picked one up that was a nice, round, leather one that was a bit larger than my outstretched hand. Then we went to the front of the store, studiously avoiding looking at the massive array of other toys that we did not want to even contemplate due to our complete embarrassment.

A cute twenty-something checker completely nonchalantly rang us up and invited me to a "Fifty Shades of Grey" night that the shop was doing for women who wanted to learn more about BDSM. I took the flier, attempting to be cool and not mortified, and my husband and I giggled like twelve-year-olds for a solid hour afterward. That paddle is still our favorite paddle, with my husband remarking that sometimes the sex shops know best. The downside to a leather paddle is that it can't travel (unless you're brave enough to have it inspected by TSA in front of a line of strangers), and you have to hide it well because it's only used for one thing.

Heavy wooden spoon: We have a few of these that I use in the kitchen, and wowzah, these hurt! They have a nice thud that you feel deeply, but I can't imagine getting more than five or six strokes with this; it does smart!

Wooden Paddle: This is similar to a heavy wooden spoon, and it does hurt. There's a reason that schools have used these for years - think the spanking scene from *Dead Poet's Society*. I've never had a serious spanking with one, but a lick or two will light up your backside.

Belt: The belt takes some skill to wield because it is a lot more flexible and can wrap around the bottom to the hip. It also can concentrate a lot of power at the tip of the swing, so you have to be careful. Belts can leave welts if not used carefully as well. The belt has some of the same benefits as the hairbrush, however, in that it can be readily available and easily portable while traveling as it is not a suspicious thing to have with you. My husband always wears a belt, and I can tell you that I get a little thrill every time he pulls it out of his pants and doubles it to put it down for the night.

Ambiance

Before I got married, I got some advice about what a healthy sex life looks like and compared it to eating food. It said the bulk of your sex life should be like your home-cooked meals - good, wholesome, connected food. There's room for some fast food, as long as there's not too much of it. And of course, you want to have some gourmet meals as well. I think the same is true for kinky sex. For me, because spanking is sort of like a short circuit to an orgasm for me, I can have a quickie and be pretty satisfied with it in a way that I never could have done it before spanking. However, having the bulk of encounters with my husband to be quickies aren't good for him or me - it's not a good connection. So instead, we try for the bulk of our encounters to make home-cooked food, wholesome and connected, with laughter and fun, and take a good amount of time for a weeknight. This might involve a pretty nightgown if I have a moment to slip one on, but that's about it.

But then there's date night, and a few times a year, there's our night away. These are the times that I write out or at least think out scenarios, sometimes wear costumes or new negligee, have a nice dinner, and have a long, satisfying encounter that leaves my bottom a little sore and my body completely relaxed.

So much of this kink is a mind game, and it is supposed to be enjoyed. What turns you on in a scenario is deeply personal, and it can hopefully be fun and something you and your partner can create together.

Noise Issues

If you are trying not to be overheard, somewhere that you are trying to keep the noise down, I have a few tips that can help. First, think noise cancellation - white noise machines, fans, washing machines, etc. If you have a smart speaker, you can have it play water sounds or something like that. Second, use implements that are quieter - such as the heavier wooden spoon, spatula, or strap (not doubled). Third, put on some thumping music. I particularly like a band with bagpipes and a heavy drum beat, and it would be pretty hard to hear anything over that! One unexpected side effect from this, however, is that whenever I see them in concert, it puts me, well, in a certain mood.

Glossary

Aftercare - The care given to the recipient of a BDSM activity after the activity; it can often include cuddling, reassurance, sex, and/or massage. It is usually a helpful thing for both parties.

BDSM - Shorthand for Bondage, Discipline, Sadism, and Masochism. This term covers a wide array of behaviors, some involving sex and some not, which include role-playing, bondage (tying or handcuffing someone), impact play (spanking, whipping, etc.), power exchange, body modification, or acting in a dominant/submissive role. In reality, it can involve anything in the kink scene.

Bondage - The kink of tying or restraining your partner, using ropes or handcuffs or similar.

Buttplug - A toy that is, well, a plug that is for your anus.

Coming out - The process of telling people in real life about something that you find central to your identity or orientation but that you have kept secret.

Consent - The agreement from both parties that what they will participate in is agreeable. Consent can be withdrawn at any time with the use of a safeword.

Dominant/submissive - This is the role in which one person (D) is the instigator of what happens in an interaction, and one person (s) is the receiver of what happens in the interaction. These terms are interchangeable with "top" or "bottom."

Ethical Expression - An outward expression of an inward truth that is within the boundaries of your core beliefs

Fanfiction - A story or other work of literature written by a fan of and including characters of a particular movie, book, or television show.

Feminism - The radical belief that men and women are created to be equal co-heirs and partners in the world.

Implement - Something you use to strike a person's bottom with during a spanking

Kink - An atypical sexual behavior.

Kinky - A person who experiences an atypical sexual identity.

Lube or lubricant - An artificial substance that provides lubrication for sexual activity. Brands such as KY or Astroglide are common.

Orientation - A person's pervasive and enduring sexual identity.

Orgasm - An intense, pleasurable reaction centered in the genitals that is the climax of sexual activity, which in a male usually leads to ejaculation and in the female leads to contractions of the clitoris and vagina.

Paraphilia - What psychology classifies as abnormal sexual desires, especially ones considered dangerous or extreme.

Safeword - An agreed-upon codeword that ends all play immediately when the play has gotten too much for the submissive partner to handle. The benefit of using a codeword is that if you want to do a scene where there are protests, there can be a way to stop the play without interfering with being able to do that sort of scene. A common word is "red" like a stoplight, with the benefit that the submissive can say "yellow" if they are getting close to having to say "red." It is considered bad manners for the dominant to force a submissive to use their word very often; it should be a very rare event.

Scene - An agreed-upon time for BDSM activities, often with a script or plan of activities.

Sex-positive - A movement that encourages a tolerant and progressive view of sex in society.

Sin - Anything that separates you from the love of God or from His people.

End Notes

Chapter 1

1. Laura Ingalls Wilder and Garth Williams, *Little House in the Big Woods* (New York: HarperCollins, 1953).
2. Justin J Lehmiller, "Is BDSM/Kink a Hobby or a Sexual Orientation?," Psychology Today (Sussex Publishers), accessed September 24, 2019, https://www.psychologytoday.com/us/blog/the-myths-sex/201905/is-kink-leisure-activity-or-sexual-orientation.
3. Jillian Keenan, *Sex with Shakespeare* (Place of publication not identified: Harpercollins, 2017).
4. Brad Sagarin, "The Surprising Psychology of BDSM," n.d., https://www.psychologytoday.com/us/blog/the-wide-wide-world-psychology/201502/the-surprising-psychology-bdsm.
5. Mark Driscoll and Grace Driscoll, *Real Marriage: the Truth about Sex, Friendship & Life Together* (Nashville: Thomas Nelson Publishers, 2013).

Chapter 2

6. 1 Corinthians 7:5
7. 1 Corinthians 7:1-5

Chapter 3

8. *Diagnostic and Statistical Manual of Mental Disorders: DSM-5.* Arlington, VA: American Psychiatric Association, 2017.
9. Brad Sagarin, "The Surprising Psychology of BDSM," n.d., https://www.psychologytoday.com/us/blog/the-wide-wide-world-psychology/201502/the-surprising-psychology-bdsm.
10. Meg Barker, Alessandra Iantaffi, and Camel Gupta, "Kinky Clients, Kinky Counselling?," *Feeling Queer or Queer Feelings?*, April 2014, pp. 106-124, https://doi.org/10.4324/9781315824390-8.
11. Nele De Neef et al., "Bondage-Discipline, Dominance-Submission and Sadomasochism (BDSM) From an Integrative Biopsychosocial Perspective: A Systematic Review," *Sexual Medicine* 7, no. 2 (2019): pp. 129-144, https://doi.org/10.1016/j.esxm.2019.02.002.

12. Meg Barker, Alessandra Iantaffi, and Camel Gupta, "Kinky Clients, Kinky Counselling?," *Feeling Queer or Queer Feelings?*, April 2014, pp. 106-124, https://doi.org/10.4324/9781315824390-8.

13. Ummni Khan, "Sadomasochism in Sickness and in Health: Competing Claims from Science, Social Science, and Culture," *Current Sexual Health Reports* 7, no. 1 (2015): pp. 49-58, https://doi.org/10.1007/s11930-014-0039-1.

14. Kolmes, K., Stock, W. & Moser, C. (2006). Investigating bias in psychotherapy with BDSM clients. In P. Kleinplatz, & C. Moser, (Eds.) *SM: Powerful Pleasures.* (pp. 301-324) Binghamton, NY: Haworth Press

15. Ummni Khan, "Sadomasochism in Sickness and in Health: Competing Claims from Science, Social Science, and Culture," *Current Sexual Health Reports* 7, no. 1 (2015): pp. 49-58, https://doi.org/10.1007/s11930-014-0039-1.

Chapter 4

16. Maneesha Deckha, "Pain as Culture: A Postcolonial Feminist Approach to S/M and Women's Agency," *Sexualities* 14, no. 2 (2011): pp. 129-150, https://doi.org/10.1177/1363460711399032.

17. Maneesha Deckha, "Pain as Culture: A Postcolonial Feminist Approach to S/M and Women's Agency," *Sexualities* 14, no. 2 (2011): pp. 129-150, https://doi.org/10.1177/1363460711399032.

18. Maneesha Deckha, "Pain, Pleasure, and Consenting Women: Exploring Feminist Responses to S/M and Its Legal Regulation in Canada through Jelineks the Piano Teacher," *Harvard Journal of Law & Gender* 30, no. 2 (2007): pp. 425-459,

Chapter 5

19. Brad Sagarin, "The Surprising Psychology of BDSM," n.d., https://www.psychologytoday.com/us/blog/the-wide-wide-world-psychology/201502/the-surprising-psychology-bdsm.

20. J.a. Talbott, "Adverse Childhood Experiences and the Risk of Premature Mortality," *Yearbook of Psychiatry and Applied Mental Health* 2011 (2011): pp. 161-162, https://doi.org/10.1016/s0084-3970(09)79276-x.

21. Scott A McGreal, "BDSM, Personality and Mental Health," Psychology Today (Sussex Publishers), accessed October 1, 2019, https://www.psychologytoday.com/us/blog/unique-everybody-else/201307/bdsm-personality-and-mental-health.

22. Scott A McGreal, "BDSM, Personality and Mental Health," Psychology Today (Sussex Publishers), accessed October 1, 2019, https://www.psychologytoday.com/us/blog/unique-everybody-else/201307/bdsm-personality-and-mental-health.

Chapter 6

23. Christian C. Joyal, Amélie Cossette, and Vanessa Lapierre, "What Exactly Is an Unusual Sexual Fantasy?," *The Journal of Sexual Medicine* 12, no. 2 (2015): pp. 328-340, https://doi.org/10.1111/jsm.12734.

24. Amanda Arnold, "The Bottom Line: Why People Love Spanking So Much," Vice, September 14, 2016, https://www.vice.com/en_us/article/paede7/the-bottom-line-why-people-love-spanking-so-much.

25. Tanya Bezreh, Thomas S. Weinberg, and Timothy Edgar, "BDSM Disclosure and Stigma Management: Identifying Opportunities for Sex Education," *American Journal of Sexuality Education* 7, no. 1 (2012): pp. 37-61, https://doi.org/10.1080/15546128.2012.650984.

Chapter 7

26. E. L. James, *Fifty Shades of Grey* (New York: Vintage Books, a division of Random House LLC, 2015).

27. Debra Soh, "COMMON BDSM MYTHS: IT'S NOT A NEW FAD, IT'S NOT VIOLENT AND NOT EVERYONE WHO PARTAKES IS PSYCHOLOGICALLY MALADJUSTED," *The Independent*, October 21, 2015,

Chapter 8

28. Jillian Keenan, *Sex with Shakespeare* (Place of publication not identified: Harpercollins, 2017).

Chapter 9

29. Meredith Bennett-Smith, "Spanking For Jesus? Fringe Christian Group's Controversial Tactics," HuffPost (HuffPost, June 21, 2013), https://www.huffpost.com/entry/christian-domestic-discipline-spanking-jesus-marriage_n_3479646.

30. Brandy Zadrozny, "Spanking for Jesus: Inside the Unholy World of 'Christian Domestic Discipline," The Daily Beast, January 1, 2017, https://www.thedailybeast.com/spanking-for-jesus-inside-the-unholy-world-of-christian-domestic-discipline?utm_campaign=Feed: thedailybeastarticles (The Daily Beast - Latest Articles)&utm_medium=feed&utm_source=feedly.

Chapter 10

31. 1 Corinthians 7

Chapter 11

32. *Strictly Ballroom* (M&A Productions, 1993).
33. Tanya Bezreh, Thomas S. Weinberg, and Timothy Edgar, "BDSM Disclosure and Stigma Management: Identifying Opportunities for Sex Education," *American Journal of Sexuality Education* 7, no. 1 (2012): pp. 37-61, https://doi.org/10.1080/15546128.2012.650984.

Chapter 12

34. Emily Nagoski, *Come as You Are: the Surprising New Science That Will Transform Your Sex Life* (New York: Simon & Schuster Paperbacks, 2015).
35. Sigmund Freud, *Three Essays on the Theory of Sexuality* (Hogarth P.;Institute if Psycho-analysis, 1962).
36. James G. Pfaus et al., "The Whole versus the Sum of Some of the Parts: toward Resolving the Apparent Controversy of Clitoral versus Vaginal Orgasms," *Socioaffective Neuroscience & Psychology* 6, no. 1 (2016): p. 32578, https://doi.org/10.3402/snp.v6.32578.
37. Mark Driscoll and Grace Driscoll, *Real Marriage: the Truth about Sex, Friendship & Life Together* (Nashville: Thomas Nelson Publishers, 2013).

Bibliography

Arnold, Amanda. "The Bottom Line: Why People Love Spanking So Much." Vice, September 14, 2016. https://www.vice.com/en_us/article/paede7/the-bottom-line-why-people-love-spanking-so-much.

Barker, Meg, Alessandra Iantaffi, and Camel Gupta. "Kinky Clients, Kinky Counselling?" *Feeling Queer or Queer Feelings?* April 2014, 106–24. https://doi.org/10.4324/9781315824390-8.

Bennett-Smith, Meredith. "Spanking For Jesus? Fringe Christian Group's Controversial Tactics." HuffPost. HuffPost, June 21, 2013. https://www.huffpost.com/entry/christian-domestic-discipline-spanking-jesus-marriage_n_3479646.

Bezreh, Tanya, Thomas S. Weinberg, and Timothy Edgar. "BDSM Disclosure and Stigma Management: Identifying Opportunities for Sex Education." *American Journal of Sexuality Education* 7, no. 1 (2012): 37–61. https://doi.org/10.1080/15546128.2012.650984.

Deckha, Maneesha. "Pain as Culture: A Postcolonial Feminist Approach to S/M and Women's Agency." *Sexualities* 14, no. 2 (2011): 129–50. https://doi.org/10.1177/1363460711399032.

Deckha, Maneesha. "Pain, Pleasure, and Consenting Women: Exploring Feminist Responses to S/M and Its Legal Regulation in Canada through Jelineks the Piano Teacher." *Harvard Journal of Law & Gender* 30, no. 2 (2007): 425–59. https://doi.org/10.1107/s0108270113015370/sk3488sup1.cif.

Diagnostic and Statistical Manual of Mental Disorders: DSM-5. Arlington, VA: American Psychiatric Association, 2017.

Driscoll, Mark, and Grace Driscoll. *Real Marriage: the Truth about Sex, Friendship & Life Together*. Nashville: Thomas Nelson Publishers, 2013.

Freud, Sigmund. *Three Essays on the Theory of Sexuality*. Hogarth P.;Institute of Psycho-analysis, 1962.

James, E. L. *Fifty Shades of Grey*. New York: Vintage Books, a division of Random House LLC, 2015.

Joyal, Christian C., Amélie Cossette, and Vanessa Lapierre. "What Exactly Is an Unusual Sexual Fantasy?" *The Journal of Sexual Medicine* 12, no. 2 (2015): 328–40. https://doi.org/10.1111/jsm.12734.

Keenan, Jillian. *Sex with Shakespeare*. Place of publication not identified: Harpercollins, 2017.

Khan, Ummni. "Sadomasochism in Sickness and in Health: Competing Claims from Science, Social Science, and Culture." *Current Sexual Health Reports* 7, no. 1 (2015): 49–58. https://doi.org/10.1007/s11930-014-0039-1.

Kolmes, K., Stock, W. & Moser, C. (2006). Investigating bias in psychotherapy with BDSM clients. In P. Kleinplatz, & C. Moser, (Eds.) *SM: Powerful Pleasures*. (pp. 301-324) Binghamton, NY: Haworth Press

Lehmiller, Justin J. "Is BDSM/Kink a Hobby or a Sexual Orientation?" Psychology Today. Sussex Publishers. Accessed September 24, 2019. https://www.psychologytoday.com/us/blog/the-myths-sex/201905/is-kink-leisure-activity-or-sexual-orientation.

McGreal, Scott A. "BDSM, Personality and Mental Health." Psychology Today. Sussex Publishers. Accessed

October 1, 2019. https://www.psychologytoday.com/us/blog/unique-everybody-else/201307/bdsm-personality-and-mental-health.

Nagoski, Emily. *Come as You Are: the Surprising New Science That Will Transform Your Sex Life*. New York: Simon & Schuster Paperbacks, 2015.

Neef, Nele De, Violette Coppens, Wim Huys, and Manuel Morrens. "Bondage-Discipline, Dominance-Submission, and Sadomasochism (BDSM) From an Integrative Biopsychosocial Perspective: A Systematic Review." *Sexual Medicine* 7, no. 2 (2019): 129–44. https://doi.org/10.1016/j.esxm.2019.02.002.

Pfaus, James G., Gonzalo R. Quintana, Conall Mac Cionnaith, and Mayte Parada. "The Whole versus the Sum of Some of the Parts: toward Resolving the Apparent Controversy of Clitoral versus Vaginal Orgasms." *Socioaffective Neuroscience & Psychology* 6, no. 1 (2016): 32578. https://doi.org/10.3402/snp.v6.32578.

Sagarin, B. (n.d.). The Surprising Psychology of BDSM. Retrieved from https://www.psychologytoday.com/us/blog/the-wide-wide-world-psychology/201502/the-surprising-psychology-bds

Soh, Debra. "COMMON BDSM MYTHS: IT'S NOT A NEW FAD, IT'S NOT VIOLENT AND NOT EVERYONE WHO PARTAKES IS PSYCHOLOGICALLY MALADJUSTED." The Independent, October 21, 2015. https://www.independent.co.uk/life-style/love-sex/common-bdsm-myths-its-not-a-new-fad-its-not-violent-and-not-everyone-who-partakes-is-psychologically-a6702396.html.

Strictly Ballroom. M&A Productions, 1993.

Talbott, J.a. "Adverse Childhood Experiences and the Risk of Premature Mortality." *Yearbook of Psychiatry and Applied Mental Health* 2011 (2011): 161–62. https://doi.org/10.1016/s0084-3970(09)79276-x.

Wilder, Laura Ingalls, and Garth Williams. *Little House in the Big Woods*. New York: HarperCollins, 1953.

Zadrozny, Brandy. "Spanking for Jesus: Inside the Unholy World of 'Christian Domestic Discipline." The Daily Beast, January 1, 2017. https://www.thedailybeast.com/spanking-for-jesus-inside-the-unholy-world-of-christian-domestic-discipline?utm_campaign=Feed: thedailybeastarticles (The Daily Beast - Latest Articles)&utm_medium=feed&utm_source=feedly.

About the Author

The Author lives with her husband of almost 20 years, more children than she had ever thought possible, and in general loves her life. She has worked as a health worker, a pastor, and is now a psychotherapist specializing in trauma. She sees her mission in life as helping people feel safe, grow in their love of God, and to find healing in relationships. In this book she has tried to be transparent and honest about the area of her life that has caused the most shame, in order to encourage freedom and peace for others.